Roberta MacLaren

30 Walks with sketch maps

COUNTRYSIDE BOOKS

*Countryside Books' walking guides cover most areas of England and
Wales and include the following series:*

*County Rambles
Walks For Motorists
Exploring Long Distance Paths
Literary Walks
Pub Walks*

A complete list is available from the publishers

First Published 1980
by Frederick Warne Ltd

This completely revised and updated edition
published 1992.

COUNTRYSIDE BOOKS
3 Catherine Road
Newbury, Berkshire

ISBN 1 85306 168 9

Sketch maps by the author

Cover photograph: Chesil Beach from Wears Hill
taken by Bill Meadows

Publishers' Note

At the time of publication all footpaths used in these walks were
designated as official footpaths or rights of way, but it should be borne in
mind that diversion orders may be made from time to time.
Although every care has been taken in the preparation of this Guide,
neither the Author nor the Publisher can accept responsibility for those
who stray from the Rights of Way.

Produced through MRM Associates Ltd., Reading
Typeset by Wessex Press Design & Print Limited, Warminster
Printed in England by J. W. Arrowsmith Ltd., Bristol

Contents

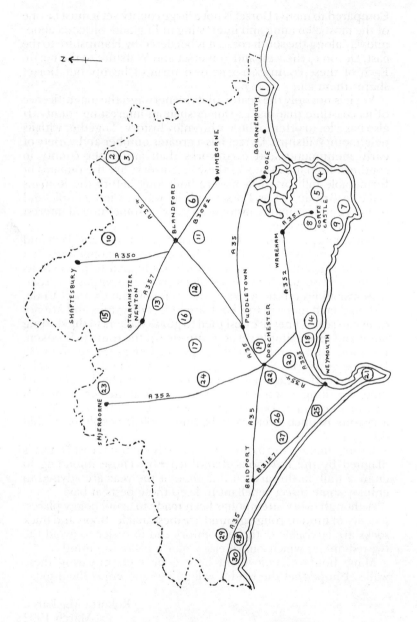

Sketch Map showing location of walks.

Introduction

Compared to many, Dorset is not a large county yet it must be one of the most charming and interesting in England. Situated about midway along the south coast, it is bordered by Hampshire to the east, Devon to the west and Somerset and Wiltshire to the north. Each of these counties has its own form of beauty but Dorset shares them all.

Yet it is not only the beauty of its scenery and the magnificence of its coastline that makes Dorset such an interesting county. It also has a lot to offer to those who enjoy history. Together with its neighbour Wiltshire, Dorset has a greater number and variety of early monuments and earthworks than any other county in southern England. Many of these earthworks are the remains of formidable hill forts which were built long before the Romans came to Britain. Thus Dorset with its wide variety of splendid scenery and fascinating history can provide something of interest for almost everyone.

With the exception of the quarrying in Purbeck and Portland and the industry in Poole, Dorset is predominantly an agricultural county. This fact, which has helped to preserve its beauty and so much evidence of its past, also imposes certain responsibilities on the walker. Always follow the Country Code.

The sketch maps in this book are in fact diagrams and are not drawn to scale. They are designed to guide walkers to the starting point and give a simple yet accurate idea of the route to be taken. For those who like the benefit of detailed maps the relevant OS Landranger Series Sheet is given at the beginning of each walk.

All the cliff paths used in the walks were perfectly safe at the time of writing, but it is never wise to walk at the very edge of a cliff or to climb it. Dorset cliffs are inclined to be crumbly and accidents happen every year because foolish people do stupid things.

Unfortunately, during spring and early summer, east Dorset is plagued by the notorious Blandford Fly. Those intending to enjoy a walk in this area at that time of the year are advised to employ some insect repellant to keep these pests at bay.

Although every attempt has been made to avoid boggy places, patches of mud or rough ground are inescapable. Boots and thick socks are advisable both for comfort and in order to avoid the twisted ankles which can so easily mar a pleasant outing.

Many hours of enjoyment have gone into preparing these walks. I hope that the reader will go out and enjoy them too.

Roberta MacLaren
March 1992

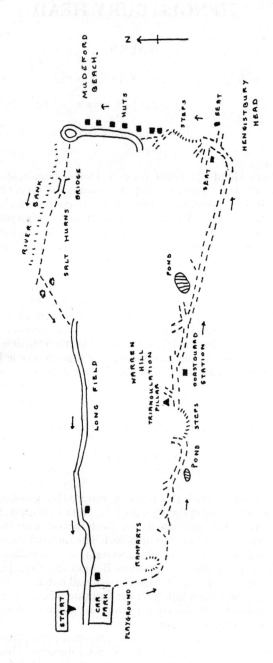

HENGISTBURY HEAD

WALK 1

★

3 miles (4.5 km)

OS Landranger 195

Hengistbury Head is a relatively new Dorset beauty spot having come into the county from Hampshire during the recent boundary changes. It is a lofty headland covered with open heath and forms the southern border of Christchurch Harbour. This is a particularly beautiful stretch of water which provides a sheltered haven for a variety of small sailing dinghies and other pleasure craft. Swans abound here and heron are sometimes to be seen amongst the reeds which line the water's edge.

Christchurch Harbour is the estuary of two large rivers: the Avon, which flows through Hampshire, and a Dorset river, the Stour. Their waters meet at Christchurch and flow on from there through Christchurch Harbour to the sea. Good views of this piece of water are to be obtained from the top of Warren Hill whilst, in the opposite direction, Poole Bay curves west towards Poole Harbour.

Hengistbury Head has not always been the deserted stretch of grass and heathland that it is today. In fact there were settlements here up until the end of the 5th century when the Saxons founded the town of Christchurch further up the river. The earliest inhabitants were a tribe of reindeer hunters who came from the Continent about 11,000 years ago and camped amongst the sand-dunes which then covered Warren Hill. Their chief concern was that their settlement was close to a ford used by the reindeer, but later settlers chose to live here for a very different reason.

Being bordered on three sides by water, Hengistbury Head is easy to defend. During the Iron Age the pair of ramparts known as Double Dykes was built across the western end, thus turning the whole headland into a promontory fort. The ramparts were built by a tribe called the Durotriges who also built the formidable ramparts at Maiden Castle near Dorchester. Behind the Double Dykes a sizeable town flourished. It grew into a small but active port which served as an important link with the Continent but was eventually abandoned during the 4th century when the number of Saxon raids on the south coast increased.

From central Bournemouth follow the signs to Southbourne and where Wentworth Avenue meets Southbourne Grove in a T-junction turn right. Carry on until the shops are left behind and

7

the road curves to the right. Here you will find the first of a series of road signs that indicate the way to Hengistbury Head. Just before the road ends there is a large car park on the right.

Leave the car park by the gap in the bank at the rear left-hand corner and head diagonally right across the children's playground. This will bring you to a wire fence which encloses the end of the ramparts. At the end of this fence turn left on to a gravel path that leads between the ramparts and the beach.

Follow this path straight ahead and where it divides keep to the right-hand fork. This crosses a stretch of grass and then joins another track that leads up a slope. At this point there are good views to the left. The Stour and Avon estuary can be seen with Christchurch Priory in the distance.

At the top of the slope the path merges with another and swings to the right. Continue along it passing a small pond on the right and then climb up the steps to the triangulation pillar. From here bear right to pass the coastguard station on your right.

Just beyond the coastguard station the path divides. Keep to the right-hand fork which leads straight ahead. This will bring you to where two tracks cross. Turn right and go down a slope, passing a pond in the valley on the left. This narrow, steep-sided valley is part of an old ironstone quarry which was dug in the middle of the 19th century.

Ignore the path to the left on the far side of the valley and continue to follow the one straight ahead. It will eventually bring you to the top of the cliffs at the end of the headland. Follow the path round to the left, ignoring a branch which leads to a seat on the right and two other branches to the left, and descend the steps to the beach.

At the bottom of the steps bear left to pass behind the beach huts. Then, where the path forks, keep to the right. This will bring you to a narrow metalled lane. Follow it straight ahead to its end and then turn left to skirt the edge of the water on your right. This is Christchurch Harbour.

Cross the wooden bridge and carry on along the rather indistinct path that follows the water's edge. Just before the river bank swings left and becomes scrub-covered, turn left on to a narrow path that leads through the undergrowth. Follow this path to where it joins the lane and turn right. This will eventually bring you back to the road and the car park.

PENTRIDGE

★

4 miles (6 km)

OS Landranger 184

Pentridge is a tiny hamlet hidden away in the rolling downland of Cranborne Chase. From the top of Pentridge Hill there are glorious views. To the south the walker can look across the valley towards Cranborne, whilst to the north the panorama of hills and dales which make up the area where Dorset and Wiltshire meet stretches away to the distant horizon.

Bokerley Ditch marks the border between Dorset and Hampshire. It was built during late Roman times to protect the area against invasion from the north-east and at one time actually blocked the old Roman road that runs across the Chase.

For those who have a few moments to spare, Pentridge church, which marks the starting and finishing point of the walk, is well worth a visit. On the left-hand side of the aisle is to be found a memorial tablet to Robert Browning, who died in 1746 and was the poet's great-grandfather.

Although there is no reason why you should not take your dog on this walk, parts of it skirt Martin Down National Nature Reserve where, for obvious reasons, dogs must be kept strictly under control.

The only metalled road to Pentridge is a narrow lane which leaves the A354, Blandford to Salisbury road, between Handley Hill roundabout and Woodyates. It is on the right coming from Blandford and is clearly marked. The lane winds its way down the hill to the village and turns sharp right at a point where another, minor lane joins it from the left. Keep following the lane round to the right, pass Trantridge Cottage on the left and then turn right opposite a large wooden barn on to a track which leads up to the church. Park on the edge of the grass to the right just beyond the church.

Go back down the track to the lane and turn right. At the end of the wall on the left, turn left to cross a stile and bear diagonally right, passing a tree on the right, to reach another stile at the corner of the wood.

Cross the stile and follow the footpath straight ahead. It runs between hedges and, in the height of the summer, can become

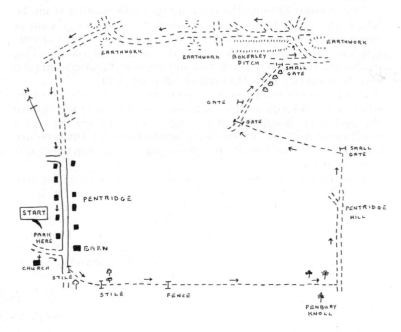

rather overgrown but it is short and never impassable. At the far end a three bar fence gives access to the open downland on Pentridge Hill.

Go straight up the hill to the group of fir trees on Penbury Knoll. There is no path but it is an easy climb. When you reach the trees, carry on through them and turn left on to a track which follows the fence. The track soon leaves the trees and runs along the ridge giving good views to left and right.

Eventually the track becomes indistinct and divides. Ignore the left-hand branch which follows the curve of the ridge and go straight on along the fence. This will lead you to a small gate in the corner of the field. Do not go through it but turn left beside it to follow the fence.

In the far corner of the fence is a gate. Go through it and follow a rather indistinct track straight ahead.

Within a very short distance this will bring you to a second gate. Do not go through it. Pass to the right of it and follow the fence on the left. This will eventually lead you down a narrow path between the fence and a line of bushes. Pass a gate on the left and carry on to another, smaller gate in the bottom left-hand corner of the field. Go through this and turn right on to the track beyond.

After a short distance the track merges with another from the left. Turn sharp left on to this and follow it down through a line of ramparts to where it divides four ways. Take the extreme left-hand fork that follows the side of the earthwork. This earthwork is Bokerley Ditch and you are now walking along the county boundary with Hampshire on your right.

Pass two other tracks on the right to reach a place in the valley where the track you are following is crossed by another. Ignore this and carry straight on up the slope. The track cuts through a small earthwork and winds along beside Bokerley Ditch before swinging right to climb another slight slope. At the top two tracks cross. Turn left.

The track cuts through the earthwork, passing a National Nature Reserve sign on the left, then runs between fields for some distance before swinging left and dividing. Take the left fork. It gradually becomes more distinct and eventually merges with a lane. Follow the lane straight ahead to where it joins the major lane at Cross Cottage and then carry straight on to reach the track on the right that leads up to the church and your car.

CRANBORNE CHASE

WALK 3

★

5½ miles (8.5 km)

OS Landranger 184 and 195

Cranborne Chase is an area of open downland to the east of Blandford. It is a beautiful place, very similar in character to Salisbury Plain and equally well endowed with archaeological remains. Besides the profusion of Bronze Age round barrows which stud its fields there are a number of other interesting earthworks, one of which is Ackling Dyke.

Ackling Dyke is the Roman road that once ran between Old Sarum and Badbury Rings. It is one of the best examples of an embanked Roman road in the country. In places the bank is over 6 ft high and a few of the old Roman milestones are still to be seen on the top of it.

Cranborne Chase gets its name from the fact that it was once a royal hunting preserve. It was first set aside for this purpose by William the Conqueror and the restrictions he imposed on the pursuit of game in the area were not lifted until 1828.

During the 18th and 19th centuries these unpopular restrictions were the cause of a great deal of lawlessness. Bands of poachers armed with vicious jointed cudgels roamed the Chase and often came to blows with the keepers. Many of these poachers were not poor people who went poaching from necessity but wealthy young bloods who resented the ban on hunting and considered poaching an exciting and permissible alternative.

Some of the countryside to be enjoyed on this walk belongs to the Shaftesbury Estate and for 30 years was in the care of the estate manager, John Ironmonger. He had a deep affection for the land in his charge and when he died his son erected a stone to his memory at Harley Gap. This beautiful spot with its magnificent views across the Chase was his father's favourite part of the estate.

Another interesting feature to be seen on this walk is the haunted barrow which stands on the ridge of Bottlebush Down. One winter evening in the late 1920s an archaeologist named Dr Clay was driving home this way from Bournemouth when he noticed a horseman coming towards him across the fields. On reaching the verge the rider turned his mount and galloped along parallel to the car waving something threateningly in his right

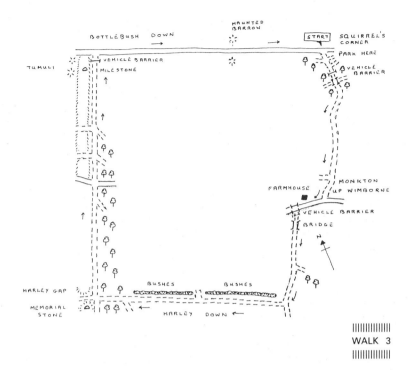

hand. To his astonishment Dr Clay suddenly realized from the way the man was dressed that what he was seeing was not a modern horse rider but an ancient Briton carrying a weapon. His professional interest aroused he studied the figure intently but, to his disappointment, as the car drew level to the barrow, the apparition vanished. Since that time several people have seen the ghostly warrior. On one occasion two young girls returning from a dance in Cranborne even reported him to the police. They thought he was a man intent on molesting them.

Take the A354 from Blandford heading towards Salisbury and turn right at the Handley Hill roundabout on to the B3081, which is signposted Ringwood. Follow this road for just over a mile to reach a point where a wood on the right approaches the road. Just beyond the first group of trees there is a track. This is Squirrel's Corner. Turn right on to the track and park on the grass beside it.

Begin the walk by ignoring two tracks on the left and one on the right and taking the track which leads straight ahead through the vehicle barrier. It goes into the wood, passes a gate on either side and then emerges from the trees to become grass-covered as it winds its way between fields.

13

After some distance the wheel ruts become more distinct and the track leads down a slope. Near the bottom it is joined by another track which comes from some farm buildings on the right. Ignore this and carry straight on to reach the lane.

Turn right and follow the lane as it curves past a white farmhouse on the right. Directly opposite the farm entrance a track leads away through a vehicle barrier on the left. Take this track. It crosses a bridge over a stream and then climbs a hill. Near the top an entrance on the left leads into a plantation of young trees but ignore this and carry straight on to where the track merges with another from the right.

Turn right on to this and follow it along the ridge keeping the bushes on your right. Ignore a grassy track which leads down the slope to the right and carry straight on towards a belt of trees. The bushes on the right are quite dense for most of the way but the occasional field entrance affords good views across the Chase.

Follow the track up to the trees and pass through them, disregarding a grassy track to the left which skirts the wood. On the far side of the trees the track is crossed by another and then passes through a dip in the bank straight ahead. This is Harley Gap and the memorial stone to John Ironmonger is to be seen set into the bank on the left-hand side of the track.

Do not go through the gap. Turn right just before it and follow the track down the hill beside the wood. Near the bottom of the slope a track emerges from the trees on the right. Ignore it and carry straight on to reach the lane.

Cross over and take the grassy track straight ahead. To the left of it is a fence bordering a tall bank covered with bushes. This bank is part of the old Roman road known as Ackling Dyke.

For some distance the track is sandwiched between Ackling Dyke on the left and a plantation of young deciduous trees on the right. It is crossed by a track which emerges from a field on the left but ignore this and carry straight on, passing a stand of young yew trees on the right to reach a place where a second track cuts through the bank and leads away to the right. Disregard it and continue to follow the one which climbs uphill beside the Roman road.

At the top of the slope there are two tumuli in the field to the left. These are some of the Bronze Age round barrows that are to be found in such great numbers on the Chase. Beside them, on the ridge of Ackling Dyke, is a Roman milestone but its surface is so weathered that the inscription is completely illegible.

Not far beyond this spot the track joins the road. Cross over and turn right to walk along the wide expanse of grass on the far side. This will bring you to where the haunted round barrow almost blocks the verge. The ghost is usually seen beside the road on the far side of it. Be brave. Skirt the tumulus and carry straight on. This will eventually bring you to a point opposite the track where you left the car.

STUDLAND

WALK 4

★

4¼ miles (6.5 km)

OS Landranger 195

During the 16th century Studland was notorious for its pirates; today it is a popular seaside village. There are two beaches, the more southerly being smaller and stonier than its counterpart which is a wide expanse of soft golden sand. The sea is perfectly safe for bathing and the sheltered harbour provides an excellent anchorage for the multitude of small pleasure craft which visit the area during the summer.

The headland which separates Studland Bay from Swanage Bay possesses some of the most beautiful coastal scenery in the whole of Dorset. It is here that the high chalk hills which separate the Isle of Purbeck from Dorset's eastern heathland come to the sea. The last part of this line of hills is Ballard Down. It forms the backbone of the headland and from the top of it there are panoramic views across Poole Harbour and Swanage.

Ballard Down ends in the tall white cliffs of Ballard Point. To the north of this the cliffs stretch away to Handfast Point where the two stacks called Old Harry and Old Harry's Wife stand in the sea. This is a paradise for bird watchers. Gulls, cormorants and other sea-birds nest on the stacks and cliff ledges whilst rooks and a variety of finches frequent the fields.

Part of this walk passes through a National Trust Downland Restoration Project and dogs should be kept on leads in the area around Handfast Point both for their own safety and to avoid any disturbance to grazing livestock.

Take the A351 from Wareham to Purbeck and turn left opposite Corfe Castle on to the B3351 signposted 'Studland'. Having travelled along this road for about 4 miles you pass a turning on the left marked 'Woodhouse Hill'. Not far beyond this there is an unmetalled lay-by on the right which is marked by a board advertising the Bankes Arms Hotel. Park here.

Start the walk by going back along the road for about 50 yards to where a path leads down a bank to the left. It is marked 'Footpath to Swanage'.

At the bottom of the bank there is a stile. Climb over this and head diagonally right to reach a second stile at the bottom of the

15

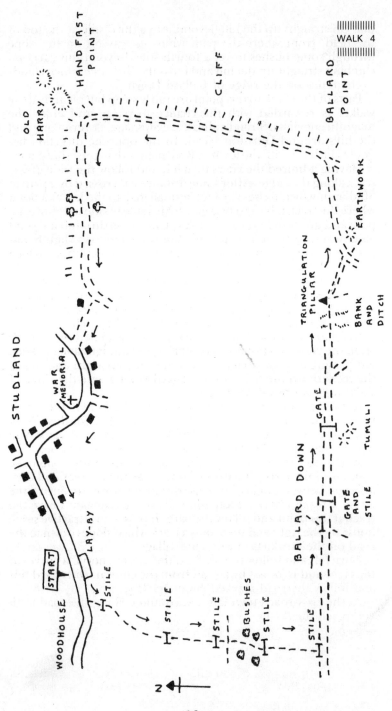

OLD HARRY

HANDFAST POINT

CLIFF

BALLARD POINT

STUDLAND

WAR MEMORIAL

EARTHWORK

TRIANGULATION PILLAR

BANK AND DITCH

BALLARD DOWN

GATE

TUMULI

GATE AND STILE

START

WOODHOUSE

LAY-BY

STILE

STILE

STILE

STILE

BUSHES

STILE

STILE

N

16

hill. Go straight up the hill beyond it to a third stile at the top of the field, from where the path winds its way on up the slope through some bushes to yet a fourth stile. Beyond this carry on climbing straight up the hill and cross the fifth stile which stands in the fence on the ridge of Ballard Down.

Parts of the climb to this point are fairly steep but on arrival the walker is rewarded with the chance to pause and enjoy the magnificent views. Straight ahead are Swanage, Peveril Point and the hills around Durlston Head. In the opposite direction lies Poole Harbour with the town of Bournemouth in the far distance.

Having admired the views turn left and follow the wide grassy track along the ridge. After some distance it is crossed by a path to Studland, which passes through a small gate to the left at a point where the track is barred by a gate with a stile beside it. Ignore the path and go straight on along the track to pass through a second gate near two tumuli. After this the track narrows slightly but keep following it straight ahead, ignoring a second track which diverges from it to the right.

Just beyond this point the track dwindles to a path for a short distance to cross a bank and ditch, beyond which is a triangulation pillar. At the pillar the track broadens once more as it bears slightly right and a path leads away beside the ditch.

Keep to the track. Within a few yards it is joined by another from the right at a point where a path goes straight ahead. Turn left passing a small circular earthwork on your right and follow the track down the hill. This is Ballard Point where the ridge of Ballard Down meets the sea.

At the bottom of the slope follow the track round to the left. It runs north along the top of the cliff towards Handfast Point where the two stacks known as Old Harry and Old Harry's Wife may be seen straight ahead as the track descends a slope.

At the bottom of the slope the track swings left to follow the contour of the coast. It passes through a group of trees and then leads on between fields for some distance before turning to the left at a place where a footpath leads straight ahead. Leave the track at this point and follow the path. It passes an attractive stone house on the right and then joins a track which slopes down to the road on the outskirts of Studland village.

Turn left and follow the road. At the war memorial it curves to the right and is joined by a road from the church. Disregard this and follow the road marked 'Swanage 3½'.

At the crossroads turn left and continue along the road until you reach the lay-by.

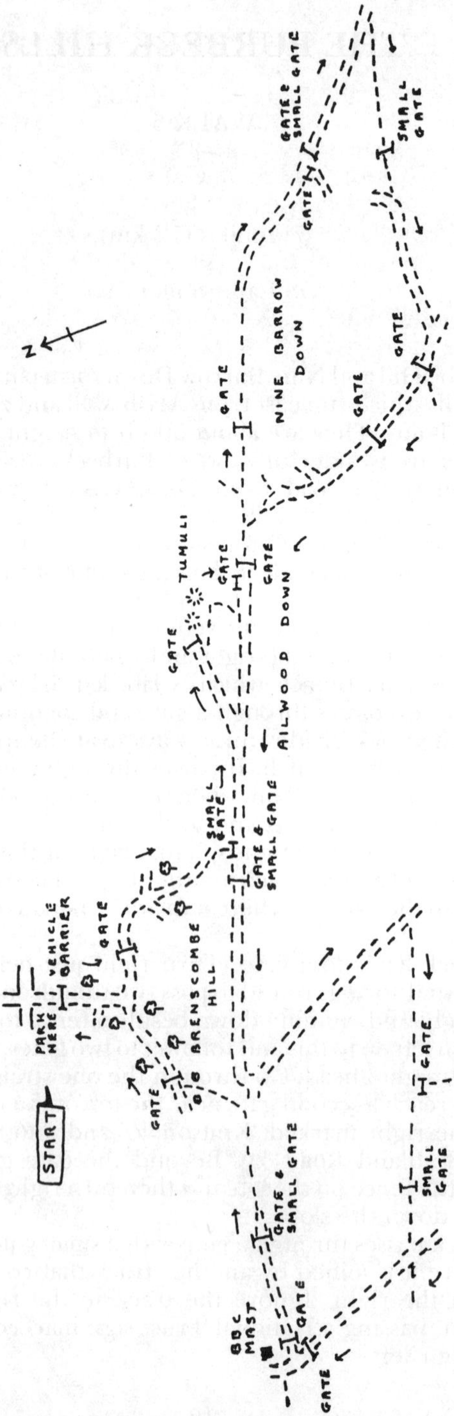

N

START

PARK HERE

VEHICLE BARRIER

GATE

OLD BRENSCOMBE HILL

GATE

BBC MAST

GATE

GATE

GATE & SMALL GATE

GATE

SMALL GATE

GATE & SMALL GATE

SMALL GATE

SMALL GATE

GATE & SMALL GATE

AILWOOD DOWN

GATE

GATE

GATE

TUMULI

GATE

GATE

GATE

GATE

GATE

NINE BARROW DOWN

GATE

GATE

SMALL GATE

GATE

SMALL GATE

THE PURBECK HILLS

WALK 5

★

7½ miles (12 km)

OS Landranger 195

Brenscombe Hill and Nine Barrow Down form part of the barrier of chalk hills which run east from Arish Mell and end in the cliffs at Ballard Point. They are about 500 ft in height, and from the ridge there are wonderful views of Purbeck.

Take the B3351 road from Corfe Castle travelling towards Studland. After about 2 miles a road to Rempstone Farm leads away to the left. Directly opposite it is a gravel track. Turn on to this and park on the right beside it. This is the foot of Brenscombe Hill.

Pass through the gap beside the vehicle barrier and carry on up the track. Ignore a track to the right and where the main track forks take the left-hand branch which is labelled 'Ulwell 2½'. It soon leaves the trees, passes through a gate and continues up the hill.

Where the track divides three ways near the top of the slope keep to the middle branch. It passes through another group of trees to reach the ridge, from where there are good views of Poole Harbour and Brownsea Island to the left.

On the ridge the track ends. Turn right at this point and go through a small gate to reach another track. Turn left and follow this track up the slope to where it divides, then take the left-hand fork.

This track leads to a gate. Turn right just before it on to a narrow path. It swings round to pass two tumuli on the left before curving right and running down beside a fence to join a further track. Turn left on to this and follow it to two gates, one on the left and one straight ahead. Go through the one straight ahead and walk on to reach a second gate near the top of the rise, ignoring a path to the right marked 'Knitson ½' and another to the left marked 'Studland Road ¾'. Beyond the gate go straight on, following the fence on the left and then turn right on to the track that leads down the slope.

The track passes through a gate with a small gate beside it, at a point where it is joined by another track that comes through a gate from the right. Ignore the track to the right and carry straight on, passing a National Trust sign marked 'Godlingston Hill' on your left.

Near the bottom of the slope the track is joined by another from the right. Turn sharp right on to this. It is marked 'Underhill Path Corfe 3¼'.

The track quickly degenerates into a path and initially follows the fence on the left. It passes through a small gate and then comes to an end at a point where a track descends the hill on the right. Follow this track straight ahead along the valley.

Where the track joins another from the left carry straight on, following the sign 'Corfe 2¾ Nine Barrow Down ¼'. The track goes through a gate beyond which a path leads away to the left. Ignore it and follow the track up a slope.

The track passes through a gate and continues to climb for a short distance before dividing. Keep to the left fork which leads straight ahead. As the track curves to the right it divides again. Take the left-hand branch. It will bring you to a signpost on the ridge of the down where the track joins another at right-angles. Turn left and follow the track through a gate.

Ignore a gate to the right and carry straight on, disregarding the path on the right by the tumuli. The track merges with another from the right, passes a small gate on the right and then runs down a slope to a gate with a small gate beside it. Go through the gate and follow the track on along the ridge. This will eventually give you good views of Corfe Castle straight ahead.

Where the track divides near a sign marked 'Corfe 1¼, Studland Rd ½, Rempstone 1' keep to the left-hand branch that leads down into the valley. Near the bottom of the slope it is joined by a path from the right labelled 'Corfe'. Turn right on to this and follow it along the foot of the hill.

Ignore a bridleway to Woolgarston which leads through a gate to the left and carry straight on. The path passes through a small gate, beyond which there are more good views of Corfe Castle, and is then crossed by a track. Turn right to follow the track up the hill.

At the top the track passes through a gate and merges with a track from the right which skirts the small enclosure containing Rollington Down BBC Mast. Turn sharp right on to this track, which is labelled 'Ridge Path Ulwell 2¾'. It passes through a gate and then runs between fields for some distance to reach another gate with a small gate beside it. After this the track quickly dwindles to a path that continues to follow the crest of the hill.

Not far beyond where the fence on the left ends, there is a stone sign beside the path. Turn left at this point and cross the grass to take a narrow path that leads down the slope through the gorse bushes to a track. Turn right and follow the track through a gate and into the trees.

After a short distance the track is joined by another from the right and then leads on down the slope. Ignore a track to the left and carry straight on to reach the place where you parked the car.

BADBURY RINGS

WALK 6

★

5 miles (8 km)

OS Landranger 195

Badbury Rings is an Iron Age hill fort protected by three concentric sets of ramparts and ditches. It commands a view which stretches from the Purbeck hills in the west to Cranborne Chase in the east and was once an important tribal stronghold. Legend has it that it was the Mount Badon where King Arthur defeated the Saxons.

An avenue of beech trees lines the road to Blandford which runs past the west side of Badbury Rings. It was planted over a hundred years ago and stretches for 2 miles from the gates of Kingston Lacy park to what used to be the edge of Kingston Lacy estate.

The avenue is said to have been set out so that the amount of trees on one side represented the number of days in a year and those on the other the number in a leap year. If this was the original intention it is unfortunately no longer the case.

Near to the gates of Kingston Lacy house stands Lodge Farm, a medieval hunting lodge dating from the 14th century. It was probably built for John of Gaunt — a younger son of Edward III and father of Henry IV - and was originally designed as a semi-defensive building having both its great hall and solar on the first floor. Lodge Farm is often open to the public and amongst the interesting features to be seen here are the remains of wall paintings and one of the finest medieval oak screens in the country.

The expanse of grass that borders Badbury Rings is a conservation and sheep grazing area where dogs are not allowed. However, any dog owners who wish to take their pets on this walk may do so by the simple process of ignoring the first two paragraphs of walking instructions which begin 'Leave the car park' and simply following the track that leads from the car park back to the road and turning left.

To reach the Rings, take the B3082 from Wimborne travelling towards Blandford. This is the road on which the beech avenue is situated. Just over half-way along the avenue a brown sign indicates the entrance to Badbury Rings on the right. The turning gives access to a well defined track that leads up a slight slope to a large parking area.

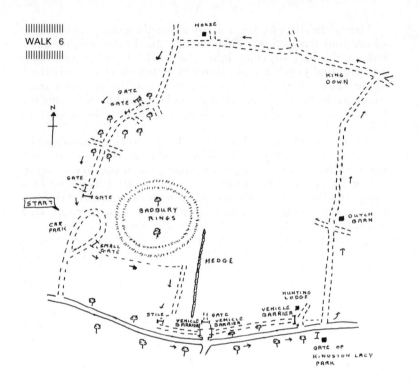

Leave the car park by the small gate on the right-hand side and walk round the base of the hill fort in an anti-clockwise direction. This will take you across the top of the wide expanse of grass which divides the rings from the road and will eventually bring you to the place where the outer rampart meets the hedge.

Just before this point a faint grassy track leads down the slope to the right. Take this track and, as it approaches the road, bear slightly right to cross a stile in the fence. Turn left on to a grassy track which borders the beech avenue.

This will bring you to a small car park at a point where a gravel track marked 'Bridleway' leads away to the left. Ignore this track and carry straight on, keeping the beech trees on your right.

Where the beech avenue comes to an end and the gates of Kingston Lacy park are to be seen on the right, the track meets another in a T-junction. Just to the left at this point there is a small house. This is the medieval hunting lodge and, if it is open, it is well worth pausing for a short while to visit it.

To continue the walk, cross the track that forms the head of the T and go on along the verge keeping the road on your right to reach a second track marked 'Bridleway'. Turn left on to this.

After some distance you will come to a place near a Dutch barn where four tracks meet. Take the one that leads straight ahead, passing the barn on your right. The track winds between fields and eventually ends in a junction where there is a lane and a track to the right and another track to the left. Take the left-hand track which leads down a slope and then forks. Keep left, following the branch that goes more or less straight ahead up the next slight hill.

On the far side of the hill the track dips down towards a white house, beside which it is joined by another track from the right. Ignore this and carry straight on, passing the house on your right.

Not far beyond the house, at a point where it is joined by a grassy track from the right, the track turns sharp left and climbs a hill. At the top it comes to a wood. Turn right here on to a secondary track that leads away through the trees.

Ignore a track which emerges from a field entrance on the right and carry straight on. Having passed a turning to the left marked 'Private' you will come to a place where two tracks cross. Go straight ahead and within a very short distance you will emerge from the trees.

Continue to follow the track as it leads down a hill and passes through a gateway on to the open grassland surrounding Badbury Rings. The car park is straight ahead at the top of the slope.

WORTH MATRAVERS
AND ST ALDHELM'S HEAD

WALK 7

★

5 miles (8 km)

OS Landranger 195

Worth Matravers is one of the most beautiful of the Purbeck villages. It is an old quarrymen's village and the famous Purbeck stone has been quarried here since Norman times. The lovely grey stone cottages and the ancient church are built of it and the hills around the village are honeycombed with quarries, some still in use and others, like those at Winspit, deserted long ago.

St Aldhelm's Chapel, which stands on the cliff at St Aldhelm's Head, is a quaint little Norman building named after a local saint who became the first Saxon Bishop of Sherborne. During Norman times a priest lived a lonely life here combining his religious duties with those of a coastguard.

From the cliff tops beyond St Aldhelm's Chapel some of the most beautiful views of the Dorset coast are to be seen and it was partly for this reason that the Dorset Branch of the Royal Marines Association chose Emmetts Hill as the site for a war memorial. The memorial, which consists of a picnic table and benches backed by a commemorative plaque, was erected in 1990 to the memory of the Royal Marines killed since 1945 in the Middle and Far East, the Falklands and Northern Ireland, and those who died in the bomb attack at The Royal Marines School of Music at Deal.

Although the area through which this walk passes is particularly beautiful it is also rugged and parts of it present some stiff climbs.

Take the B3069 from Kingston travelling towards Langton Matravers and a mile beyond the outskirts of Kingston turn right on to a lane signposted 'Worth Matravers'. Ignore a car park on the right and drive on to pass the *Square and Compass* on the left. At the junction just beyond it turn right and then take the first turning on the right, passing the duck pond on your left. Follow this lane for ¾ mile to where it turns sharply right at Rempstone Farm and then turn left on to a gravel track which leads through the farmyard to a car park on the right.

Leave the car park by the small gate in the right-hand corner of the wall and turn right to walk along the track for a very short

24

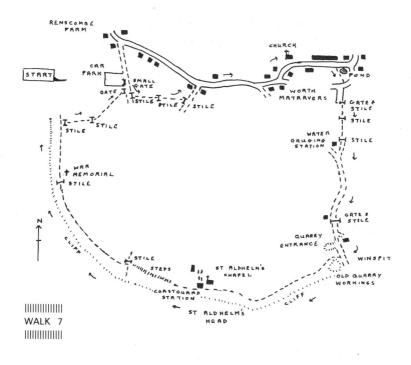

distance before turning left to cross a stile on to a footpath. The path follows the fence on the right to reach another stile at the far side of the field and then continues to a third stile which gives access to a track. Turn left, follow the track up to the lane and then turn right.

The lane leads back to the village. Ignore a track to the right marked 'Footpath to Winspit' and carry straight on, bearing left to pass the church.

Just before the T-junction turn right on to a path which passes to the right of the duck pond and leads down to another lane. Turn right and then almost immediately left into a cul-de-sac marked 'Footpath to Winspit'.

In the left-hand corner at the far end there is a stile with a small gate beside it. Go over the stile and follow the footpath down the hill, crossing two more stiles. After the third the path widens and within a short distance joins a track at a point where there is a small water gauging station on the right-hand side. Turn left and follow the track down through the valley.

After about ¼ mile a gate bars the way but, should this be locked, there is a stone stile beside it. Cross this and continue to follow the track. Before long it will curve to the left. A small cottage nestles in the valley on your left and directly opposite, on the right, is an old quarry entrance sealed off with a grating. Just beyond this on the right the fence comes to an end and a narrow path leads up to the cliff top.

The first part of this path is steep but it is a short climb, and at the top the walker is rewarded by a magnificent view down across the old quarry workings to the tiny inlet of Winspit, from where the coastline curves round to the lighthouse near Durlston Head.

Follow the path along the cliff top. It is fairly narrow but easy walking and quite safe provided you remember to keep well away from the edge. After about a mile the fence which borders the path turns inland and the path forks. Take either branch, they both lead up the short slope and join again at the top where you will see St Aldhelm's Chapel and the coastguard station straight ahead of you.

It is well worth pausing for a while to visit the tiny chapel, which is an almost unique survival of a series of similar buildings that once served as landmarks and lookout posts along our coasts. Then, from the coastguard station, continue along the cliff path which is marked at this point 'Chapman's Pool 1¼ miles'.

Within a hundred yards you will come to a flight of steps cut into the side of the hill. The view from the top is breath-taking and must be one of the best to be seen on the whole of the Dorset coast.

Descend the steps. At the bottom the path is crossed by another that leads over a stile to the right. Ignore this and go up the slope marked 'Coast path Chapman's Pool 1'. It is a stiff climb but at the top there are more superb views. The path passes the little cove called Chapman's Pool on the left and comes to a stile. On the far side of this the Royal Marine War Memorial is surrounded by a fence on the right. It is possible to enter the enclosure, where a table and benches have been provided for the use of visitors but please be sure to leave the site as clean and tidy as you would wish to find it.

From the war memorial the path leads on along the cliff top, skirting the wall on the right to where a stile marked 'Renscombe ½' gives access to a path. Turn right to cross the stile and follow the path to a second stile. On the far side of this bear slightly left across the next field to reach a gate that opens on to a track. The car park is on the left.

CORFE CASTLE

WALK 8

★

5 miles (8 km)

OS Landranger 195

The Isle of Purbeck is one of the most beautiful parts of the county. It is a place of softly rolling hills, picturesque grey stone villages and magnificent views. The beginning and end of this walk give you the opportunity to enjoy some of the best of these views. In the outward direction, the walker can see the wide expanse of water that is known as Poole Harbour. This is the second largest natural harbour in the world. It is dotted with densely wooded islands and bordered on the Purbeck side by open heathland. On the far shore the ancient port of Poole and the town of Bournemouth are to be seen on the horizon.

The return journey along the ridge affords the walker equally good views in the opposite direction. This time the panorama takes in the village of Church Knowle and the hills around Swyre Head with the sea in the distance.

Corfe Castle is one of the most beautiful of the Purbeck villages; a place steeped in history and tradition and dominated by the ruins of its ancient castle.

Take the A351 from Wareham travelling towards Swanage. At the outskirts of Corfe Castle turn right on to the road to Church Knowle, Steeple and Kimmeridge. Having passed through Church Knowle village turn right again at the crossroads on to a narrow lane signposted 'Stoborough 3½, Wareham 4¼'. The lane climbs a hill between high banks, passing the cottages which make up the tiny hamlet of Cocknowle. It turns left, slightly left again and then sharp right at the top of the slope. At this point a track leads straight ahead and it is possible to park on the left near where it leaves the road.

Go back down the hill for a short distance and, ignoring a footpath to the left labelled 'East Creech ¾', take a track signposted 'Ridge Path Corfe Castle 1¾' which leads straight up the hill. Follow the track on along the ridge, passing a memorial stone to Mary Baxter MBE on the left.

This will bring you to another gate. Go through it and straight on to reach a gate at the far side of the field. From here follow the narrow path. It veers slightly to the right across the hillside,

27

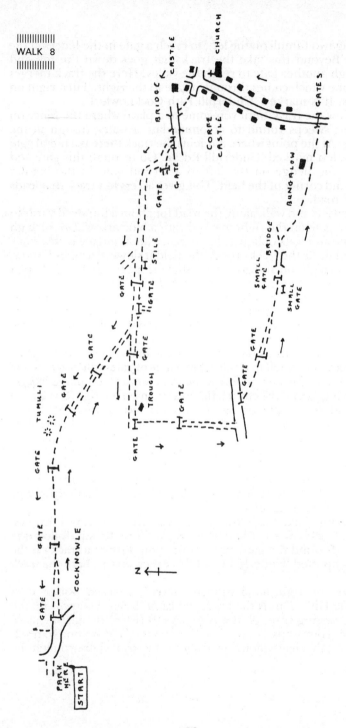

passing two tumuli on the left, to reach a gate in the fence on the right. Beyond this take the track that goes down the hill and through another gate to reach the valley. Here the track merges with one which comes through a gate to the right. Turn right on to this. It is marked 'Underhill Path Cocknowle 1'.

Follow the track until you come to a place where the fence on the left sweeps round to accommodate a water trough in the hedge. At the point where it rejoins the track there is a metal gate on the left marked 'Underhill Rd ½'. Go through this gate and follow the hedge on the left to a second gate in the bottom left-hand corner of the field. This gives access to a track that leads to the road.

Turn left and walk along the road for about a hundred yards to reach a gate on the right marked with a blue arrow. Go through the gate and walk obliquely left to reach another gate with a track beyond it. As the track crosses the field it slowly becomes fainter. Carry straight on and go down a slight slope to reach a U-shaped extension in the far corner of the field.

Leave the field by a small gate half hidden amongst the bushes in the right-hand corner of this extension. Beyond it the path leads over a small humpbacked bridge and then divides. Take the right-hand fork which goes up the slope.

The path winds its way through some bushes and then passes a bungalow on the left to reach a semi-circle of gates which give access to the road. Turn left to follow the road down through the village.

Having passed the church the road turns to the right but ignore this and go straight on for a short distance to turn left into a cul-de-sac. At the end of this a path leads away to the right. It skirts the castle mound and then emerges on to the road.

Turn left to cross the bridge and then right through a gate marked 'Bridleway Knowle Hill ¾'. On the far side of the gate bear left to follow the track. It leads up a slight slope, curves to the right and forks. Keep to the right-hand branch. It leads up a slope and then forks again.

This time take the left-hand branch which is marked 'Knowle Hill ½ Cocknowle 1¼' and, ignoring a stile to the left, follow it to a gate. Beyond the gate carry straight on. Ignore a track on the left signposted 'Underhill Road ½' and go on to where the track forks.

Take the right-hand branch which is marked 'Ridge Path Knowle Hill'. This is the track you came down. Follow it up the slope, passing through the two gates to reach the narrow path. Retrace your steps along this and across the field beyond to reach the track that leads along the ridge to the road where you left the car.

HOUNS-TOUT
AND CHAPMAN'S POOL

WALK 9

★

4 miles (6 km)

OS Landranger 195

The village of Kingston stands high on the ridge of the Purbeck hills. It has two churches; the elder disused and in the process of being converted into a house, the younger an impressive, 19th century building which looks more like a miniature cathedral than a village church. From the village street there are fine views across the valley towards Corfe Castle.

Houns-tout Cliff, which guards the western side of Chapman's Pool, is approached along a ridge overlooking the Encombe Estate. This estate was once owned by the 1st Earl of Eldon, who was William Pitt's Lord Chancellor. The views across the valley from the ridge are quite magnificent and include an obelisk erected to the memory of Lord Eldon's brother, Lord Stowell.

Take the B3069 from Corfe Castle heading towards Langton Matravers. At the top of the hill which leads up to Kingston turn right beside the *Scott Arms*. Follow the road straight ahead. Having left the village behind, the car park for Houns-tout is on the left.

Leave the car park by the narrow path through the bushes. This is beside the noticeboard at the rear of the parking area.

Where the path joins an unmetalled track turn right. The track runs for some distance between belts of trees, swings right then left and is joined by two tracks from the right and one from the left. Ignore these and carry straight on to where the track divides. Keep to the left-hand fork which, within a short distance, divides again. This time take the right-hand fork. It leads to a field gate with a stile beside it.

Cross the stile and go straight ahead following the wall on the left. At this point the obelisk erected to the memory of Lord Stowell is to be seen on the hillside to the right.

Further along the ridge you will come to another gate and stile, beyond which keep to the track that follows the wall. After some distance this track is joined by another that comes up the hillside from the right. Disregard it and carry straight on, passing through yet another gate with a stile beside it.

30

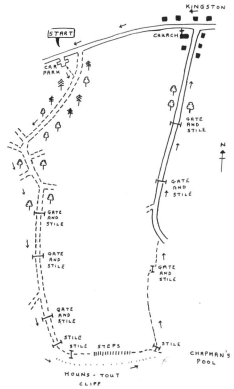

This will eventually bring you to a stile at the end of the ridge. Cross it and follow the narrow path to a second stile. Beyond this the path curves left to follow the edge of the cliff to the top of a flight of steps. At this point there are good views of Chapman's Pool in the valley below.

Descend the steps and continue down the path for some distance before turning sharp left across a stile marked 'Coast Path, Hill Bottom ¾, St Aldhelm's Head 2¾'. Bear obliquely left to follow a grassy path across the hillside to a gate with a stile beside it which is set on a raised track that cuts through the fence on the right.

Cross the stile and take a narrow path to the left that leads up to the lane. Turn left to follow the lane up the valley.

The lane climbs steadily and crosses a cattle grid with a gate and stile beside it. Beyond this it goes on for some distance before leading through another gate with a stile beside it and continuing on to Kingston village. Having passed the younger of the village's two churches on the left, the lane joins the road in a T-junction. Turn left and follow the road back to the car park.

ASHMORE

WALK 10

★

4½ miles (7 km)

OS Landranger 184

The village of Ashmore gains its name from the beautiful pond which lies at its heart, for the word Ashmore is derived from Asshemere, 'the lake by the ash trees'. This pond was once a very important stretch of water. It lay on one of the ancient trackways known as the Great Ridgeway and it very rarely dried up, thus providing a reliable watering place for wayfarers and their animals. Today it is just a pond surrounded by pretty cottages and home to a large flock of ducks.

But it is not just the pond that makes this part of the country well worth a visit. Ashmore, at 700 ft above sea-level, is the highest village in Dorset and from the surrounding countryside it is possible to see as far as the Isle of Wight and Purbeck.

Parts of this walk lead through pleasant woods where the timid woodland birds and animals are to be seen. The trees are mainly deciduous and in autumn add a riot of colour to already delightful surroundings.

Take the A350 from Blandford travelling towards Shaftesbury and turn right in Fontmell Magna to follow the road signs to Ashmore. Drive through the village to the pond and park by the war memorial on the left.

Walk back through the village. Having passed the church on your right and four garages on your left, turn left on to a gravel track marked 'Bridleway only. No motors'. This track runs between open fields along the top of the hill and affords excellent views.

Ignore one track to the left and another leading through a field gate to the right and carry straight on to where a belt of trees approaches the track from the right and there is a wood on the left. Just beyond the beginning of this wood, turn right to pass a Dutch barn on your left.

Follow the track round to the right, through a gateway and into the trees. After some distance it descends a slope, near the bottom of which there is a stile on the left. Ignore this and continue to where the track is crossed by another.

Turn left on to the cross track. At intervals it is joined by tracks from the right but disregard these and also one on the left and

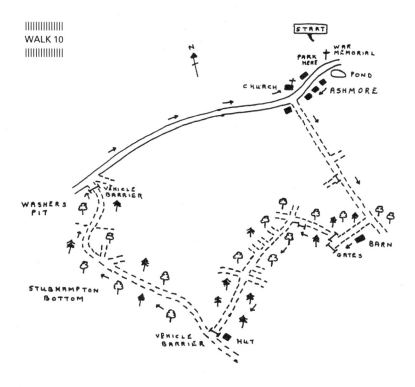

carry straight on to where the track merges with another which comes down a slope to the left. At this point a grassy track leads straight ahead. Follow this on through the trees.

After some distance the track passes through a vehicle barrier and joins a wider track in a T-junction, at a point where there is a corrugated iron hut on the left. Turn right on to the wider track and follow it through the valley. This is Stubhampton Bottom. Keep to the main track ignoring all side turnings until it eventually meets the road at Washers Pit.

Turn right and walk up the road to the village. Carry straight on, passing the church on the left, to reach the place where you parked the car.

TARRANT CRAWFORD

WALK 11

★

4½ miles (7 km)

OS Landranger 195

Tarrant Keyneston and Tarrant Crawford get their names from the little river Tarrant which flows down through the hills from Cranborne Chase to join the river Stour near Spetisbury. Tarrant Keyneston is a fairly large village with a few pretty thatched cottages whilst Tarrant Crawford consists of little more than a church and a farm. Yet in the past Tarrant Crawford was the more important of the two.

Bishop Poore, the founder of Salisbury Cathedral, was born in Tarrant Crawford and he was instrumental in establishing a Cistercian abbey here during the latter half of the 12th century. He had written one of the finest books ever composed in Middle English, the *Ancren Riwle*, or the Nun's Rule, especially for a group of anchoresses associated with Tarrant Crawford church and it was probably as a result of his interest in this community of religious women that Tarrant Abbey was founded.

Bishop Poore was one of two important people to be buried in Tarrant Abbey. The other was Queen Joan of Scotland who was a daughter of King John. Both their graves are lost beneath the grass which hides the abbey ruins but two stone coffin lids situated on either side of the altar in Tarrant Crawford church are said to have belonged to them.

Spettisbury Ring, or Crawford Castle as it is sometimes called, crowns the hill overlooking Spetisbury village. It is a hill fort composed of a single bank and ditch which was originally constructed during the Iron Age and later used as a Saxon stronghold. Part of its eastern rampart was destroyed when the railway line was built in 1860 but enough remains to display its original size and shape.

Crawford Bridge is one of the many beautiful old bridges which span the river Stour. It has nine arches and was originally constructed during the 15th century. It was restored a century later and since that time has remained virtually unchanged.

Take the B3082 from Wimborne travelling towards Blandford and turn left opposite the 'True Lover's Knot' in Tarrant Keyneston on to the road to Tarrant Crawford. Just after passing the church on the right at the far side of Tarrant Keyneston

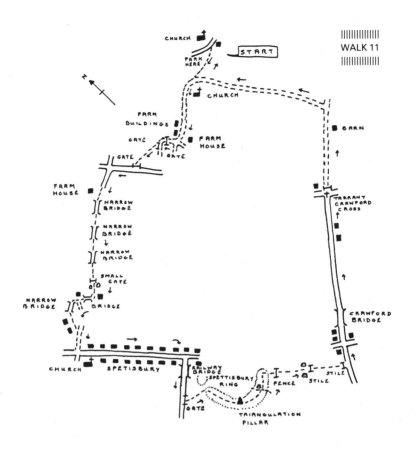

village, the road swings to the right. Park on the left at this point beside a path marked 'Bridleway Tarrant Crawford ¾'.

Walk along this path to where it joins a track and then follow the track straight ahead keeping the little river Tarrant on the right. This will lead you past Tarrant Crawford church on the left.

Beyond the church the track skirts some farm buildings on the right and then turns to the right at a point where there is a farmhouse on the left. Follow the track round to the right through a gate and then, as the track turns left once more, leave it to pass through a gate on the right-hand side which is labelled 'footpath'. Bear diagonally left across the field to reach a second gate that opens on to a lane.

Turn right to follow the lane to the crossroads and then left on to the lane marked 'Keyneston Mill'. This leads down to a farm. Pass in front of the farmhouse, which was once the old mill, and cross the river Stour by a narrow bridge. At the far side go straight ahead across the meadows following a path that passes over two more narrow bridges.

Beyond the second bridge a small metal gate will be seen set in the hedge at the far side of the field. This gives access to a path which, after winding for a short distance through bushes, goes past a house on the left and then turns right to cross a bridge. At this point the remains of the mill-race are to be seen on the right.

Having crossed the bridge turn left, ignoring a drive on the left, to cross another narrow bridge and take a path that leads past some cottages on the right to reach a track. Turn right and follow the track to the road.

Where the track joins the road turn left and walk for ½ mile through Spetisbury village to reach a lane on the right signposted 'Bridleway South Farm'. Turn right and follow the lane under the railway bridge. Beyond the bridge continue up the hill for a short distance before turning left through a field gate on to a footpath marked 'Spettisbury Ring & Middle Buildings ¾'.

Go up the slope to the earthwork. At the entrance, turn right to mount the rampart and walk round the top to the triangulation pillar. From here there are magnificent views across the surrounding countryside. To the east the Stour valley is spread out like a carpet and to the west the Purbeck hills can be seen on the horizon.

Carry on along the rampart, ignoring a path which crosses it diagonally at a point where some hawthorn bushes have encroached upon the slope. Beyond this you will come to the place where the rampart ends beside the fence. At this point turn right on to the path that leads steeply down the side of the rampart and across the ditch to a low wire fence. Step over the fence and continue along the path. It skirts the field and passes through a clump of bushes to reach a stile. Cross the stile and walk along the edge of the next field to where a second stile gives access to the lane.

Turn left and follow the lane down to the main road. Cross over and carry straight on. This will bring you to Crawford Bridge.

Continue along the road beyond the bridge until it reaches the T-junction where the old Tarrant Crawford cross stands on a grassy island amidst the diverging strips of tarmac. At this point go straight ahead to follow a gravel track through a gate.

After some distance the track forks at a point just beyond a Dutch barn on the right. Take the left-hand fork and follow it until it swings left beside the river Tarrant, then turn right on to the path which leads back to the car.

MILTON ABBAS

WALK 12

★

2½ miles (4 km)

OS Landranger 194

Milton Abbas is one of the most picturesque villages in Dorset and also one of the youngest. It was built during the latter years of the 18th century and forms a lasting monument to a rich man's despotism.

Up until that time there had been a small market town called Milton Abbas. It was situated about ½ mile away from the present village close to the ruins of Milton Abbey. Then, in 1771, Lord Milton, 1st Earl of Dorchester, had a beautiful mansion built beside the old abbey church. In spite of its situation, he wished his house to be set in spacious grounds so he ruthlessly demolished the old town to make himself a park. He rehoused the townsfolk in the new village which he had constructed on the curving slope of the Blandford road out of sight of his house.

Milton Abbey was founded in AD 932 by King Athelstan as a college of canons and later became a Benedictine monastery. The original abbey church was destroyed by fire during the 14th century and was never fully rebuilt. It has no nave because the Dissolution of the Monasteries took place before it was completed.

After the Dissolution the abbey and its property was bought by Sir John Tregonwell. It was one of his descendants, another John Tregonwell, who had a very narrow escape there during the next century when he fell from the top of the abbey church's tower. He was only five years old and had been taken to the top of the tower by his nurse. Whilst leaning over the parapet to pick a wild rose he slipped and fell. His nurse fled back down the stairs in a panic only to find her charge unconcernedly collecting daisies on the grass below. He had been saved from disaster by his nankeen petticoat which had acted as a parachute and floated him safely down to earth.

St Catherine's Chapel stands high on the hill overlooking the abbey church to which it is connected by a flight of grassy steps. The chapel is over 800 years old and was originally built as a wayfarer's chapel where travellers and pilgrims could pause to pray.

During the 19th century the chapel was used as a pigeon house

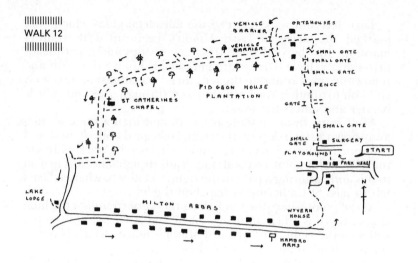

thus giving the name Pidgeon House Plantation to the wood which surrounds it. Later it was converted into a labourer's cottage, a carpenter's workshop and then a timber store. It was restored to its original use in 1901 by Everard Hambro who owned the estate at the time. Today the chapel, which is regularly used, is maintained by the boys of Milton Abbey School together with a few dedicated parishioners.

Take the A354 from Blandford travelling towards Puddletown and turn right in Winterborne Whitechurch on to the road to Milton Abbas and Bulbarrow. Follow this road for 2½ miles at which point there is a junction on the left signposted Milton Abbas. Pass this and take the next turning on the left by the bus shelter. Park on the right.

Walk on along the road for a short distance, passing one pair of semi-detached houses on your right, and then turn right on to a grassy path that leads between the gardens to a children's playground. Skirt the playground following the hedge on the right and at the lane turn left to pass the surgery on your right.

Just beyond this the lane ends. Turn right through a small gate marked 'Bridleway' and head straight across the field to a second gate on the far side. Beyond this the path leads straight ahead beside a hedge on the left.

Ignore a track to the right near the centre of the field and go straight on. The hedge on the left gives way to a wall and, after a short distance, a path leads through a gap in a fence to the left. Turn on to this path and follow it through three small gates to reach a track.

Turn left and walk between the tall metal gates which once marked the drive to Lord Milton's beautiful 18th century mansion. Just beyond them the track divides and a path leads through a vehicle barrier straight ahead. Ignore this path and follow the track round to the left, then turn almost immediately right on to another track which passes through a second vehicle barrier and enters the wood.

After some distance there is a path and then a track leading away down a steep slope to the right. Disregard both of these and continue to where, having descended a slope, the track swings to the left. At this point a second track leads straight ahead. Turn on to this and, ignoring a path to the right, follow it to where it bears left to pass St Catherine's Chapel on the left.

At the point where the track skirts the western wall of the little chapel there is a beautiful view of Milton Abbey church in the valley to the right. Part of Lord Milton's house, which is now a public school, is also just visible beside it.

On leaving the chapel carry straight on along the track, ignoring a path which leads up the hill to the left. Upon reaching the place where the track meets an unmetalled lane turn right and walk down the hill to the road. Turn left and follow the road to the T-junction.

Just before reaching it there is a cottage on the right called Lake Lodge. Beside it a path leads through some gates. This is a public footpath to Milton Abbey church and it makes a worthwhile detour for those who would like to take a closer look at this fine old building.

To continue the walk, turn left at the T-junction into the village. This is Milton Abbas. Carry straight on up the hill, passing the *Hambro Arms* on the right, to where the left-hand pavement ends outside Wyvern House. Not far beyond this a footpath leads away to the left. Turn on to it and follow it up the slope to where it emerges at the head of a cul-de-sac. Follow the cul-de-sac round to the left, and where it joins the road, turn right to walk back to the car.

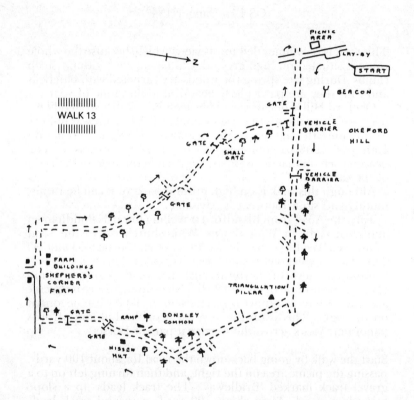

WALK 13

OKEFORD HILL
AND TURNWORTH DOWN

WALK 13

★

4½ miles (7 km)

OS Landranger 194

This walk is recommended for its views which, because the whole route is situated on high ground, can be enjoyed without steep climbs. During late spring the woods are carpeted with bluebells and thus they are particularly beautiful at that time of year.

Okeford Hill is one of the old beacon hills which stretch like a necklace along the south coast of England. A beacon was lit here to announce the sighting of the Armada in 1588 and another on 19th July 1988 to commemorate its 400th anniversary. The beacon used on that occasion is to be seen in the field to the right of the car park.

Although this walk is on high ground parts of it can be rather muddy and stout footwear is advisable.

Take the A354 from Blandford travelling towards Puddletown and turn right in Winterborne Whitechurch on to the road signposted 'Winterborne Clenston 1¾, Winterborne Stickland 3'. Travel along this road for just over 6¼ miles. This will take you through Turnworth, beyond which the road begins to climb towards the summit of Okeford Hill. Near the top there is a picnic area on the left but ignore it and park in the lay-by just beyond it on the right. This is on the very crest of the hill and affords panoramic views across the northern part of Dorset.

Start the walk by going back down the road for about 100 yards, passing the picnic area on the right, and then turning left on to a gravel track marked 'Bridleway'. The track leads up a slope towards a wood. After about 100 yards a second track leads through a gate to the right and, just beyond it, a path goes through a vehicle barrier into the woods. Ignore both these and carry straight on keeping the Forestry Commission sign marked 'Wareham Forest, Okeford Hill' on the right.

Within a short distance the track forks. Take the right-hand branch which leads straight ahead and is partly obstructed by a vehicle barrier. As the track emerges from the trees it is joined by a track on either side. Ignore both these and carry straight on. The track merges with another from the right and skirts a stand of trees on the left. Where the track divides take the right-hand fork, which passes a triangulation pillar on the right.

Keep straight on along the ridge, ignoring a track on the right, to reach the wood. Here the track is crossed by another which runs along the edge of the trees. Ignore the cross track and carry on into the trees.

At the point where the track is joined by one from the left, turn right. Ignore a track to the left and then another on the right by a concrete ramp where the main track bends left to pass a Nissen hut on the left.

Beyond this the track curves to the right, passes through a gateway and follows a hedge on the left. Then, having passed through a pair of gates and skirted a small wood on the right, it emerges on to a lane.

Turn right and follow the lane down the hill to a farm. Here, where it curves sharply left beside a cottage garden, a track leads straight ahead between the farm buildings. Leave the lane to follow this track up the hill.

On the crest it is joined by another track from the right. Turn right on to this. The first few hundred yards of it can be rather muddy but it is possible to skirt the worst patches. The track runs between fields and then enters a wood. Ignore a path to the right at the beginning of the wood and keep to the track.

At the far end of the wood it passes through a gate and becomes more indistinct. Ignore a track to the left and then one to the right and carry straight on keeping the bushes on your right. The track passes through another gate and then borders a wood on the right.

Just as the trees begin, a path leads through a small gate on the right. Turn right on to this path and then almost immediately left where the path divides to take the branch which runs through the edge of the wood.

Pass through the vehicle barrier at the far corner of the wood, ignoring a path which leads away to the right just before it, and turn left to follow the track down to the road. At the road turn right to walk back to the lay-by.

RINGSTEAD BAY
AND DURDLE DOOR

WALK 14

★

8 miles (12.5 km)

OS Landranger 194

The tall grassy hills which end in the precipitous cliffs at Swyre Head, Bat's Head and White Nothe make parts of the latter half of this walk into a series of steep ascents and descents and, although the cliff path is quite safe, this is not a walk for people who suffer from vertigo. However, for those who are fairly energetic and enjoy magnificent scenery, it is not to be surpassed. The coastline between Durdle Door and Ringstead Bay has a wild beauty all of its own. Although the land is farmed it is extremely isolated and was once a favourite haunt of smugglers who landed their cargoes on the deserted beaches. The cliffs at White Nothe provided part of the setting for *Moonfleet*, J. M. Falkner's famous novel about the Dorset smugglers.

Another author, Llewelyn Powys, lived near White Nothe during the early part of the 20th century. He loved the area so much that he expressed the wish to be buried here but initially his wishes were frustrated. He died abroad on 2nd December 1939 at the age of 55 and, owing to the war which then raged in Europe, it was impossible to return his body to Dorset for burial. He was cremated in the country where he died and his ashes were eventually brought back to England when the war was over. They were buried to the right of the track which runs across the edge of Chaldon Down and their resting place is marked by a memorial stone carved by Elizabeth Muntz.

Not far from the Llewelyn Powys memorial the work of another sculptor is to be seen. Set in stone niches cut into the bank to the right of the track are a set of beautifully carved stone shells. All of them are different and each represents the shell of a species of mollusc to be found on the local beaches.

During the first half of this walk there are fine views of the Isle of Portland and its harbour which is protected by massive stone breakwaters. These breakwaters were constructed by convict labour during the middle years of the 19th century when it was decided to establish a prison on Verne Hill.

Take the A352 Wool to Dorchester road travelling towards Dorchester and having passed through East Knighton turn left by

43

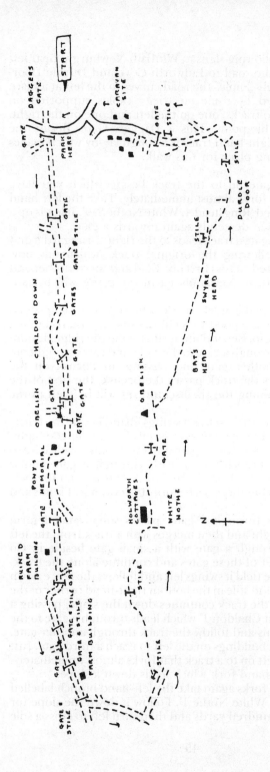

the *Red Lion* inn following signs to Winfrith Newburgh. Bear left at the church on the road to Lulworth Cove and Durdle Door. After approximately 2 miles the road curves to the left at a place where it is crossed by some electricity cables supported on wooden posts. Two tracks, one on the left and one on the right, join the road at this point. This is Daggers Gate. Beside the beginning of the right-hand track is a rough lay-by which makes an excellent parking place for this walk.

Go through the gate on to the track beside which you have parked. The track forks almost immediately. Take the left-hand fork which is marked 'Ringstead 4, White Nothe 2½'. It leads up a slight slope and then descends again towards a gate.

Just beyond this gate a track leads to the right. Disregard it and go straight on, following the original track, which has now become grass covered, across first one field and then another and ignoring a footpath to Newlands Farm camp site which leads away to the left.

In the third field the track crosses the top of a steep-sided hollow where there are good views of the sea, and then climbs a hill to a gate at the top. Beyond this it runs along the ridge. Ignore a track that leads through a gate to the right and carry straight on, going through another gate and passing an obelisk on the right-hand side. As the track passes the obelisk, the first of the stone niches containing the shell sculptures will be seen in the bank to the right.

Continue to follow the track as it swings inland beside the fence. The memorial to Llewelyn Powys is just ahead on the right. Beyond it the track curves left again and eventually divides. Keep to the right-hand branch which leads through a gate and is signposted 'Ringstead NT Sea Barn Farm'. At this point the view of the sea is hidden but there is a beautiful panorama of fields and hills to the right.

The track leads through a gate, passes some ruined farm buildings on the right and then merges with a track from the left before passing through a gate with a small gate beside it. Go through the smaller of these gates and continue along the track. At the corner of the field it swings left and follows the fence down the slope to a gate and stile in the bottom right-hand corner of the field. Beyond this the track continues down the slope, passing a track marked 'West Chaldon 1' which leads through a gate to the right. Disregard this and follow the track through another gate, passing some farm buildings on the left to reach a third gate. Just beyond this turn left on to a track that forks almost immediately. Keep to the right-hand fork which leads down a slope.

Where the track forks again take the left-hand branch labelled 'Lulworth Cove 5, White Nothe 1'. Follow it down the slope for approximately a hundred yards and then turn left to cross a stile and follow a footpath up the hillside, keeping the fence on your right. This is the beginning of the cliff path. It swings to the left and follows the edge of the cliff, passing over a stile and on to Holworth cottages.

Follow the path to the seaward side of the cottages, where it forks. The right-hand branch leads to the cliff edge so keep to the left which is marked 'Lulworth Cove 3½' and runs along beside the garden wall. Beyond this the path continues to follow the cliff top and will eventually bring you to where a gate on the left gives access to a path that goes to Daggers Gate and South Down. Ignore this and carry straight on to reach another obelisk.

Just beyond the obelisk the path forks. Take the right-hand branch which is marked 'Lulworth Cove 3'. It is wider than its counterpart and leads obliquely down the hillside.

Continue to follow the path as it leads up the other side of the valley to the ridge beyond. This is Bat's Head. Go down the steep slope on the far side, from where the path climbs once more to reach the top of Swyre Head. Here the path passes through a gap in a fence with a stile beside it before descending to the next valley.

At the bottom of the hill the path forks at a point where a path to Newlands Farm camp site crosses a stile to the left. Take the right-hand branch. It runs up a slope at the top of which another path leads away to a stile on the left. Ignore it and carry straight on. At this point there is a good view of Durdle Door which becomes even better as the path curves round to reach a place where there is a fence and a stile.

Cross the stile and follow the path to where it forks. Take the left-hand branch. It curves round to join a broad gravel track. Turn left on to this and walk up the hill, ignoring two paths to the left and another track which diverges from the main one to follow the cliff edge on the right.

Near the top of the hill there is a stile on the right but disregard it and carry on to pass through a gap beside the gate that gives access to the caravan park. From here the track leads straight ahead, passes through a gap in the hedge marked 'Caution Ramps Speed Limit 5 mph' and becomes a metalled lane. Follow it through the main part of the caravan park and up to the road. At the road turn left and walk along the verge until you reach the car.

MARNHULL

WALK 15

★

3 miles (4.5 km)

OS Landranger 183

This walk will be of particular interest to anybody who enjoys the work of Thomas Hardy. Marnhull is one of the settings that he used for his famous novel *Tess of the D'Urbervilles*. In the novel it is Marlott, the village where Tess was born and where her family lived.

As with all Hardy's stories, once you have located the place where it is set, it is possible to identify actual buildings that are described in the story. The *Crown Hotel*, which stands beside the B3092 to the east of the church, is The Pure Drop; the public house where John Durbeyfield wanted to take Parson Tringham. The *Blackmore Vale Inn* appears in the story as Rollivers, the off licence where Tess's parents enjoyed illicit drinking parties in the bedroom and, on the outskirts of the village, a delightful thatched cottage is said to have been the family's home.

Marnhull is situated in a particularly beautiful part of Dorset known as the Blackmore Vale. To the west of the village is a wide valley through which the infant river Stour meanders its way towards the sea. Here there are magnificent views towards Stalbridge in the west and Bulbarrow in the south.

Take the B3092 from Sturminster Newton heading towards Gillingham. Having passed the sign that marks the outskirts of Marnhull the road swings sharp right. Just beyond this bend a large lay-by on the right provides plenty of room to park.

Start the walk by following the road for a very short distance to where it swings left. At this point there is a gate on the right. Go through it and head diagonally left across the field to reach a stile in the hedge. This gives access to a narrow bridge across a ditch, on the far side of which is a second stile. Beyond this bear left to a gate in the fence.

Cross the stile beside the gate and turn right to head straight up the slope towards some farm buildings. This will bring you to another stile just to the right of a water trough. Cross it and head straight across the field beyond to a gate that opens on to the farmyard. Carry straight on between the farm buildings and pass through a second gate to reach the road. Cross over and turn left to

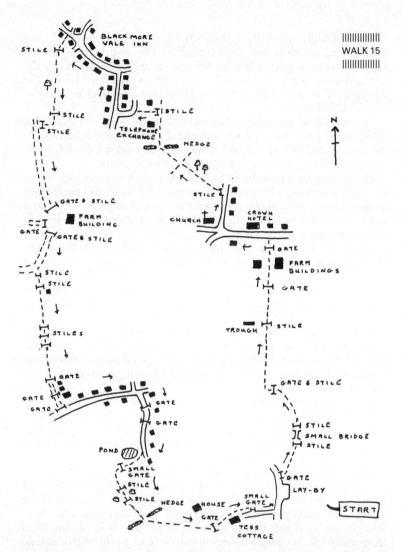

pass the *Crown Hotel* on your right. (Hardy's The Pure Drop pub.)

At the road junction by the church turn sharp right into Church Hill. At the end of the churchyard on the left, turn left to cross a stile on to a path signposted 'Footpath to Sackmore Lane'.

Head diagonally right across the field to pass a clump of small trees on your right and then carry straight on to the corner of the field, ignoring a second footpath which crosses the first at right-angles. At the corner of the field turn right to follow the path through a gap in the hedge and on across a second field, passing a red brick telephone exchange on the left. Just beyond it there is a stile on the left. Cross this and follow the path to the road.

48

Carry straight on to the T-junction, turn right to follow the road to the next junction and then turn left. This will bring you into Barton Street. It curves left, passes a surgery and car park on the left and some shops on the right and then swings right beside the *Blackmore Vale Inn*. This is the building that featured in Hardy's novel as Rollivers.

Do not follow the road round to the right. Cross over and walk along Ham Lane which leads straight ahead. Ignore a turning to the right called Woodland Mead and, just beyond it, turn left on to a footpath that cuts between some gardens to a stile.

Head straight across the field, passing an oak tree on your right, to reach a second stile in the far corner. Cross it and turn right almost immediately to go over another stile that gives access to a track. Turn left to follow the track, which provides good views of the Stour valley to the right.

The track leads to a gate and stile near some farm buildings. Cross the stile and turn sharp right to skirt the fence on the right for a short distance to where two tracks diverge. Take the left-hand track. Follow it for a short distance to where it turns right to descend the hill and then go straight on to cross two stiles set one in front of the other at the beginning of the hedge.

Head straight across the field to reach a set of three stiles and then carry on to a gate and stile on the far side of the next field. Beyond this a track leads past some corrugated iron buildings on the left to a gate that opens on to a drive. Go straight up the drive to the road.

Turn left to walk along the road and take the first turning on the right, which is just opposite a turning on the left called Kentisworth Road. Follow the lane through the gate marked 'Private road Dogs on leads' and on through a second gate, beyond which it descends a slope to where there is a pond on the right.

Bear slightly right at this point on to a narrow footpath that runs along the bank of the pond to a small gate. Go through the gate and turn left to follow the hedge on the left to a stile in the corner of the field. Pass through the bushes to cross a second stile and carry straight on to a gap in the hedge. On the far side of this head diagonally left, keeping a house on your left, to go through a gate in the hedge.

Walk straight across the next field to the corner of the hedge and then follow the fence on the right. It skirts a cottage garden. This is Tess Cottage, the fictional home of Tess of the D'Urbervilles.

Where the cottage garden ends carry on along the hedge to a small gate that gives access to the lane on the right. To the left this lane leads to the road and the lay-by where you parked the car but, before following it in that direction, it is worth turning right to make the short diversion to the cottage gate and enjoy the beautiful view of the cottage across the garden.

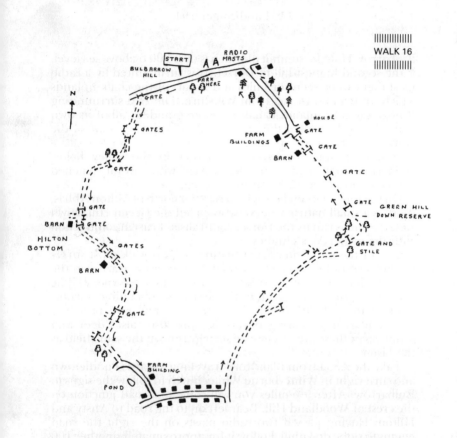

WALK 16

START
RADIO MASTS
BULBARROW HILL
PARK HERE
GATE
N
GATES
GATE
GATE
BARN
HILTON BOTTOM
GATES
BARN
GATE
FARM BUILDING
POND
HOUSE
GATE
FARM BUILDINGS
GATE
BARN
GATE
GATE
GREEN HILL DOWN RESERVE
GATE AND STILE

HILTON

WALK 16

★

4½ miles (7 km)

OS Landranger 194

Bulbarrow Hill, the summit of which is over 900 ft above sea level, is the second highest hill in Dorset. It is surmounted by a radio mast that can be seen for miles and is part of the chalk uplands which stretch into Dorset from Wiltshire. The area surrounding Bulbarrow is farmland. It has a remote grandeur all of its own and affords the walker the opportunity of enjoying some of the Dorset countryside at its best.

Hilton, in spite of its name, nestles in the valley below Bulbarrow. It is a pleasant little village with several thatched cottages and a fine 15th century church.

On the top of Green Hill, which is to the north of Milton Abbas, there is a small nature reserve. It is called the Green Hill Down Reserve and is run by the Dorset Naturalists' Trust in conjunction with the owner Mrs Hughes.

One of the most interesting features of this walk must surely be the herd of bison which are usually to be seen grazing in the fields beside the track. They belong to Mr Ellis, the owner of The Warren Farm, who created the herd by obtaining surplus stock from zoos and wildlife parks. He has built up a breeding herd and is now rearing bison. Mr Ellis also raises deer and numbers of these are often to be seen grazing in the same field as the bison.

Take the A354 from Blandford travelling towards Puddletown and turn right in Winterborne Whitechurch to follow the signs to Bulbarrow. After 5½ miles you will come to a road junction on the crest of Woodland Hill. Bear left on to the road to Ansty and Hilton. Having passed two radio masts on the right the road begins to slope downhill. Follow it for approximately another 100 yards and, just before it swings left, park on the left-hand verge beside two beech trees.

Walk on along the road for a short distance and then turn left on to a track marked 'Bridleway Hilton and Milton Abbey'. This leads through a gate, follows a hedge on the left and eventually widens at a place where there are three gates; one straight ahead and the others on either side. Go through the one straight ahead and bear obliquely right down the slope to reach the far corner of the wood on the right.

Beside it a gate opens on to a track. Follow the track down the hill to reach a barn in the valley. Go through the gate at the bottom of the slope and then through a second gate beside the barn. This is Hilton Bottom.

Beyond the gate the track swings left and it is at this point that the bison and deer are often to be seen in the field on the right. At the far end of their field the track passes through three gates beside a barn on the right and then carries on along the valley for some distance before swinging right to pass between hedges to a gate. Ignore a track which leads to a farm on the right and carry straight on.

Within a short distance the track merges with another which comes through a gate on the right. Follow it round to the left. This will bring you to where the track you are following joins a metalled one. Carry straight on along this to where it joins a lane in a T-junction. Turn left to walk through Hilton village and at the next T-junction turn left again.

This branch of the lane almost immediately degenerates into a track which leads up a slope between hedges. After a while the hedge on the right comes to an end and then the track forks. Ignore the right-hand branch which leads to a gate and carry straight on.

At the top of the hill the track bears right and a path leads straight ahead. Leave the track to follow the path, ignoring a small gate on the left. The path passes through a grove of trees to reach a gate with a stile beside it. This is the entrance to Green Hill Down Reserve.

Cross the stile and swing left to skirt a patch of brambles on the left and take a path that cuts through the bushes. After a short distance this is joined by another path from the right but disregard it and carry straight on to reach a gate. Beyond it follow the fence on the left to another gate at the far side of the field. Go through this and continue to follow the fence. It will bring you to a third gate that opens on to a track straight ahead.

The track passes a derelict barn on the left before passing through a gateway to join a metalled track at a point where there are some farm buildings on the left and a house on the right. Follow this track straight on through the trees to where it joins the road and then turn left to walk back along the road to the car.

THE DORSETSHIRE GAP

This walk is well off the beaten track and for those interested in the wild-life of the countryside it can be very rewarding. It is set in an area where a wide variety of flowers are to be seen and timid creatures such as deer, hares and foxes abound.

The Dorsetshire Gap is a deep cut through the hills between Nettlecombe Tout and Higher Melcombe which marks the place where five ancient trackways meet. It is a fascinating place, being so completely hidden from all sides that the walker comes upon it with startling suddenness.

Higher Melcombe is a tiny hamlet that nestles in a valley to the south of the Gap. Its main feature is a curious old manor house part of which was once a chapel. There has been a house on this site since Norman times and probably even earlier but the oldest portion of the present building dates from the latter half of the 16th century and is all that remains of the fine Elizabethan mansion built by Sir George Horsey.

Take the B3143 from Dorchester heading towards Sturminster Newton and as the road leaves Piddletrenthide turn right on to a lane signposted 'Plush, Mappowder'. Travel along this for just under 3 miles following the signs to Mappowder and, having passed a board on the right marked 'Folly Farmhouse' at a point where a track crosses the road, park on the verge on the right.

Start the walk by going back to the cross track and turning left. Follow the track up the hill and where it forks take the left-hand branch. This passes a stand of trees on the left and quickly degenerates into a path as it continues to climb to reach a gate.

Go through the gate and follow the path straight ahead to where the line of bushes on the left ends, then turn left to follow a track across the field to a water tank. At this point part of the earthwork that crowns Nettlecombe Tout can be seen across the field to the left.

Turn right beside the water tank and follow the hedge on the left to a gate in the far corner of the field. Beyond it the track becomes more distinct and, on a clear day, there are magnificent views across the rolling countryside to the Purbeck hills.

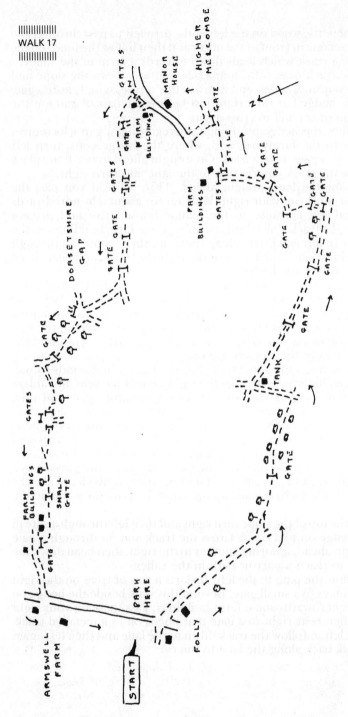

Where the wood on the left ends, turn left to pass through two gates set one in front of the other and then follow the fence on the left to a track which leads down towards a farm in the valley.

The track passes through a gate halfway down the slope and then continues to descend with a hedge on the right. Ignore a gate in this hedge but turn right just before the pair of gates at the bottom of the hill to cross a stile.

Follow the hedge on the left, disregarding a gap which gives access to the farmyard, and, where the hedge ends, turn left through a gate on to a track. Go straight ahead to reach the place where the track emerges on to the lane and turn right.

Follow the lane straight ahead. This will lead you past the manor house on your right. Walk on for about a hundred yards beyond the entrance to the manor house drive and, having ignored a track which leads between some farm buildings on the left, turn left at a point where there are three gates. Go through the middle one, which is signposted 'Dorset Gap', and bear sharp left to follow the hedge.

Ignore a track that runs through a gate on the left and carry straight on to reach a gate in the far corner of the field. Go through it, cross the end of a metalled track and pass through a gate on the far side to continue following the hedge on the left. This will bring you to a gate straight ahead that opens on to the lower end of the Dorsetshire Gap.

Go through the gate and follow the track which winds its way between high banks that, at the right time of the year, are ablaze with flowers. The track passes through another gate and then divides. Keep to the right-hand branch. It climbs a slope and eventually emerges at the place where the five trackways meet.

Take the second track on the left which is labelled 'Armswell Farm'. It quickly narrows to a path and leads down through the trees to a gate. Go through the gate and follow the grassy track straight ahead for a short distance to where it divides. Take the left-hand branch. It leads up the slope, keeping the wood on the left.

At the top of the slope turn right and then left through a gate in the hedge on to a track. Cross the track and go through a gate straight ahead, ignoring another to the right, then head down the slope to reach a narrow path in the valley.

Follow the path to the left. It skirts a row of trees on the right and comes to a small gate. Beyond this walk beside the hedge on the right towards some farm buildings. Pass these on your right and then bear right to a gate that opens on to a metalled track. Turn left to follow the track down to the lane and then left again to walk back along the lane to the car.

OSMINGTON MILLS

WALK 18

★

3 miles (4.5 km)

OS Landranger 194

Osmington Mills is one of the prettiest places on the Dorset coast. Separated from the village of Osmington by the main Weymouth road, this tiny hamlet lies in a pleasant valley through which a small stream makes its way to the sea. Osmington Mills is where John Constable came to paint his famous *Weymouth Bay*, and even today the view is almost unchanged.

Ringstead Bay, overlooked to the east by the great cliff of White Nothe, is a delightful place. One of its main claims to fame is the mystery of the old village which once stood here. It became completely deserted during the 15th century and all that remains of it today are a few grassy humps in a field. Why the village was abandoned is a mystery but there are two theories put forward to explain it. One is that the village was destroyed during a French raid in 1420 when the villagers took refuge in the church, which the marauders subsequently burnt. The other is that the population was wiped out by the Black Death.

Take the A352 from Dorchester travelling towards Wareham. Having passed through Broadmayne the road leads to a roundabout just outside the village of Warmwell. Turn right here on to the A353 which is signposted Weymouth. This will take you through Poxwell. Just beyond the village, after the road swings right, turn left on to a narrow road marked 'Ringstead 1½'. Go through Upton and park on the left-hand verge just beyond the sign on the right which marks the end of the hamlet.

Walk on along the road for a short distance. As it bends to the left there is a metalled track marked 'Upton Glen Caravan Park' leading away to the right. Turn on to this and follow it up the slope to where it forks. Take the left-hand fork. It goes through a gate with a stile beside it.

Where the track forks again keep to the right. This leads to another gate with a stile beside it. Cross the stile and carry straight on to where the track narrows and leads down to a lane.

Turn left and then almost immediately right on to a footpath that goes down a slope, following a line of trees on the left. At the bottom of the slope the path is spanned by a stile. Beyond this it

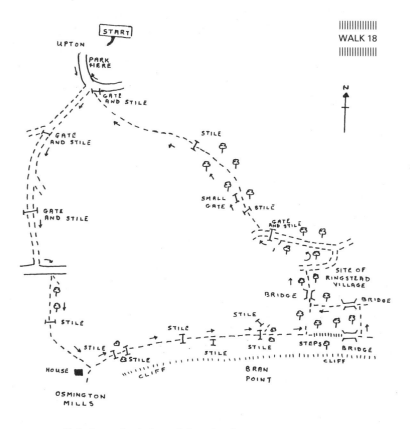

curves slightly to the left and then leads across the field, skirting a white house on the right.

At the corner of the white house's garden the path crosses a ditch and then joins another faint grassy path at right-angles. To continue the walk you must turn left here and follow the path up the slope to the cliff top but, before doing this, explore the path to the right. It leads down to the delightful little hamlet of Osmington Mills and a very short walk will take you past the pretty thatched cottages to the rocky shoreline where there are beautiful views.

Having followed the left-hand path up the slope you will come to two stiles set one in front of the other amongst some bushes near the cliff top. Cross both of these and continue to follow the path, keeping the cliff on your right.

The path leaves the bushes and leads down a slope to a stile. Cross this and continue along the path, passing another stile and descending a second slope. This will bring you to a place where there is a stile to the left and another straight ahead. Ignore the one to the left and, having crossed the other, follow the path through the bushes straight ahead, passing a second path which leads up a slight slope to the left.

Beyond the bushes the path runs beside a fence at the end of which there is yet another turning to the left. Disregard it and carry straight on, following the path down the steps through the trees.

Cross the bridge at the bottom and turn left on to a path that borders the stream. Within a very short distance it forms a T-junction with a path which crosses a small bridge. Turn left and climb the slope. At the top the path meets another. Turn right to follow it across the gully and through the woods to a metalled track, then turn right again.

The track bends to the right at a point where there is a field gate on the right opening on to a meadow. This meadow is the site of Ringstead village. Its remains lie hidden beneath the humps and hollows that are clearly visible in the middle of the field.

Continue along the track. It leads into the trees and then merges with another track from the left. Turn left on to this. Ignore a path to the left marked 'to coast path & sea' and go on along the track which is signposted 'Upton, Osm. Mills'. It passes through a gate with a stile beside it and leads down to a stream. Turn right to keep the stream on your left and cross a stile to re-enter the wood.

Follow the path up the slope, ignoring a small gate on the left. The path climbs steadily up through the wood to reach a stile at the far end of the trees. Beyond it is a field. Walk straight ahead keeping the fence on your right.

Disregard a gate in the fence and crest the ridge, from which there is an excellent view of the man on horseback that is cut into the hillside just east of Weymouth and represents King George III.

Follow the fence on the right on down the slope to reach a gate and stile which give access to the road. Turn left to walk back along the road to the car.

THE HEART OF HARDY COUNTRY

WALK 19

★

4½ miles (7 km)

OS Landranger 194

For all who know and love the works of Thomas Hardy the area around Higher and Lower Bockhampton will be of special interest. This is the true heart of Hardy country, the place where he was born, grew to maturity and wrote two of his most famous novels.

The delightful little church at Stinsford is where he worshipped as a boy. It has a window dedicated to his memory and under one of the churchyard trees his heart lies buried beside the remains of other members of his family.

Stinsford is the village of Mellstock immortalised in his novel *Under The Greenwood Tree* and in this work the church and its choir are vividly portrayed. The gallery which they used has since been demolished but the little church still retains much of the atmosphere that it must have had when Hardy knew it.

Lower Bockhampton, with its little humpbacked bridge and picturesque thatched cottages, was also a village that Hardy knew well. It was here, at the age of eight, that he began his scholastic career. He spent one year at the village school in Lower Bockhampton before going on to enter a Nonconformist school in Dorchester.

Hardy's cottage, which stands in the hamlet of Higher Bockhampton on the edge of Puddletown Forest, is a beautiful little thatched cottage. Thomas Hardy was born here on 2nd June 1840 and in it he wrote *Under The Greenwood Tree* and *Far From The Madding Crowd*. Beside the cottage stands a simple stone monument erected in the 1930s by some of the author's American admirers. Today the cottage is the property of the National Trust. Its garden is open to the public from March to October and the interior of the cottage can be seen by appointment with the tenant.

Besides the features on this walk connected to the life of Thomas Hardy, there is also an interesting little pond on the outskirts of Puddletown Forest. It is called Rushy Pond and is dependent for its water on local rainfall. Rushy Pond stands on an old smugglers' route known as 'The Snail's Creep' and it is

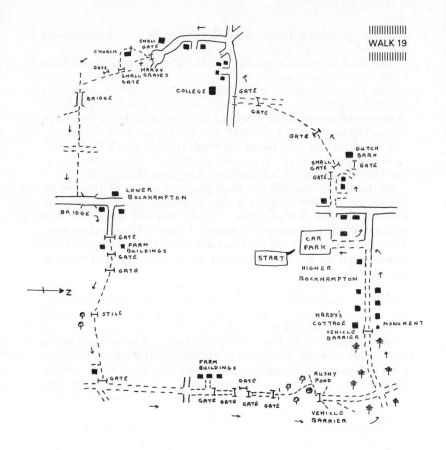

thought that smugglers used to pause here to rest and water their horses.

Leave Dorchester on the A35 heading towards Poole and where it meets the roundabout at the end of the bypass go straight across on to the road marked 'Stinsford ¼, Kingston Maurward ¼, Bockhampton 1½, Tincleton 4'. Follow this road for almost a mile and at the crossroads turn left on to a narrow road signposted 'Hardy's Cottage'. After about ½ mile this will bring you to a lane on the right marked 'Higher Bockhampton, Hardy's Cottage'. Turn right here and, within a short distance, right again on to a gravel track which leads to a car park.

Leave the car park by the way you entered it and walk back up the lane to the road. Turn left, passing two white bungalows on the left. Just beyond them a farm track crosses the road. Turn right on to this, passing a house on the left and some farm buildings on the right.

The track eventually curves to the right and ends at a Dutch barn. As it does so a small metal gate gives access to a field straight ahead. Go through this gate and follow the fence on the right down the hill to a second gate. Beyond it a narrow footpath leads obliquely right across the field to a farm track in the valley. Turn left to follow this track through two field gates to the road.

Turn right and walk along the road. It leads up a hill. Across a field to the left a large white mansion house is to be seen. This is the Dorset College of Agriculture, Kingston Maurward.

At the top of the hill the road passes a group of four white houses on the left and then dips downhill again to pass the entrance to the college drive. Not far beyond this there is a turning on the left marked 'Stinsford Church, Stinsford School'. Take this turning. It will lead you past some of the college's farm buildings on the left before curving left and then right to finish at the church.

Enter the churchyard through the small gateway. A tarmac path leads straight ahead for a short distance and then forks. The left fork runs down to the corner of the church and the right curves round behind it to end at a similar gateway in the far corner of the churchyard. The right-hand path is the one to take for it leads past the church door and enables the walker to pause for a few moments to study the interior of the church but, before doing this, take a short diversion on to the left-hand one. Beside it, to the left, are the graves of the Hardy family. Here lie buried the author's parents and his wife. She is buried together with her husband's heart. The remainder of his ashes lie in Poet's Corner, Westminster Abbey.

Having followed the right-hand path round behind the church, leave the churchyard by a small wooden gate. Turn right and follow the path which initially runs between two sections of the graveyard and then follows a metal fence on the left to a stream.

At this point the path meets another in a T-junction. Turn left and, ignoring a path to the right on the far side of the bridge, carry straight on keeping the stream on the left.

After some distance a farm track crosses the path. Disregard this and carry straight on to where the path ends at the bridge. Turn left across the bridge and, having passed a thatched cottage on the right, turn right on to a metalled track that leads to some farm buildings.

Go through the gate at the end of the track and walk across the farmyard to reach a gate on the far side. Beyond it there is another gate that gives access to a field.

Bear slightly right across the field to reach a stile beside the wood and then go straight ahead towards a white house near the right-hand corner of the field. Pass this house on your right, ignoring a path that leads down into some bushes on the right just before it, and leave the field by a gate that opens on to a track. Turn left to follow the track up to the road and then cross over on to another track that leads straight ahead. This is marked 'Pine Lodge Farm'.

The track passes some farm buildings on the left to reach a gate. Go through this and straight ahead to a second gate, beyond which a third gate gives access to a track that skirts a hedge on the left. This will bring you to a gate in the far corner of the field. It opens on to an area of open scrubland.

Just beyond the gate the path is crossed by another. Ignore it and go straight on following the path up the hill. At the top of the slope there is a pond on the right. This is Rushy Pond.

Turn right on to a narrow path which runs along the bank on the far side of the pond. Where the path joins a track turn left to pass a vehicle barrier and take the track straight ahead ignoring paths on either side.

Follow this track, ignoring a grassy path to the right, to where it passes through a stand of trees and crosses another track at right-angles. Turn left. The track leads through the wood to a vehicle barrier. Go through the gap beside it on to a gravel lane. The stone monument to Thomas Hardy is on your right and the thatched cottage on the left is Hardy's cottage.

Carry on along the lane to where it joins the metalled lane leading up to the road. Turn left and follow the gravel track back to the car park.

WHITE HORSE HILL

WALK 20

★

3½ miles (5.5 km)

OS Landranger 194

Lying on the outskirts of Weymouth, the northern part of Sutton Poyntz is a haven of peace and undeveloped beauty. Here are to be seen old thatched barns, stone cottages and a pond bordered with willow trees where a variety of ducks swim on the clear water. Osmington is another grey stone village set back from the main road. John Constable spent his honeymoon here and he was so impressed with the village that he painted it. *Osmington Village* is one of his lesser known works but it was also during his stay here that he painted the more famous picture, *Weymouth Bay*.

White Horse Hill gets its name from the large figure of a man on a horse which has been cut into the chalk of its south slope. It is a huge figure, 280 ft long and 320 ft high but, unlike many hill carvings, it is not very old. It was first cut in 1808 under the direction of a local bookseller and is a portrait of King George III on his horse. The work was done to commemorate this king's association with Weymouth. Together with his brother, the Duke of Gloucester, King George paid regular visits to the town as a result of which it grew into a fashionable and wealthy seaside resort.

Parts of this walk can be rather boggy and suitable footwear is advisable.

From Weymouth sea front follow the signs 'A353 Wareham and Wimborne'. On the far side of Preston turn left opposite a public house called *The Spice Ship* into Sutton Road. This is signposted 'Sutton Poyntz'. Follow the road to where it divides and take the right-hand fork which is labelled 'Sutton Poyntz and Springhead'. Drive up this road until you come to a public house on the right called *The Springhead*. Park opposite it on the left beside the duck pond.

Walk straight on to where the road ends and turn right on to a track marked 'Public Footpath'. Pass the joiner's yard on your left and carry straight on to reach a gate labelled 'Footpath only. No horses'. Go through this and then straight ahead through a second gate which opens on to a field.

Walk straight across the field to a gate at the far side and then

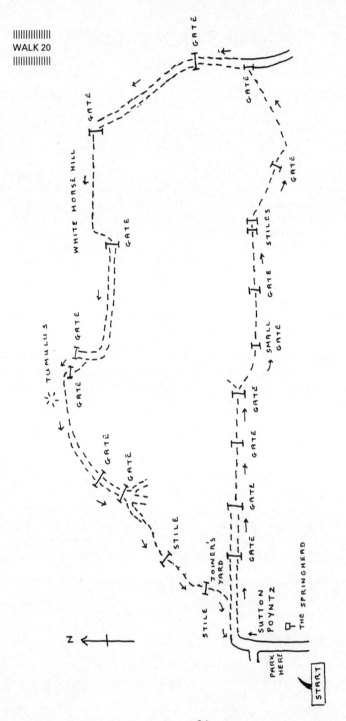

GATE

GATE

WHITE HORSE HILL

GATE

GATE

TUMULUS

GATE

GATE

GATE

GATE

STILE

STILE

JOINER'S YARD

STILE

GATE GATE

GATE

SMALL GATE

GATE

STILES

GATE

N ←

SUTTON POYNTZ

THE SPRINGHEAD

PARK HERE

START

64

continue across the next field to another gate. Beyond this a path leads away to the left. Ignore it and carry straight on, following the hedge on the right. This will bring you to a small gate in the bottom right-hand corner of the field. Go through it and straight ahead once more to reach a gate at the far side of the next field. From this field there are good views of the White Horse on the hill to the left.

Bear slightly left across yet another field to reach a double stile in the hedge and obliquely right to go through a gate on the far side of the field beyond, then follow the fence straight ahead.

Leave the fence where it turns right and carry straight on towards the houses which mark the edge of Osmington village. This will bring you to a gate in the corner of the field. Turn left to follow a track marked 'Coast Path Inland Route'. It leads between hedges to a gate and then bears left up the hillside.

At the top of the hill turn left to pass through a gate on to a path signposted 'Bincombe 2, Abbotsbury 10'. This leads straight ahead following the fence on the right. The field it is skirting lies right on the ridge of the hill and there are good views of Weymouth Bay and Portland to the left.

At the far side of the field the path curves round to a gate signposted 'Bincombe, Abbotsbury'. Go through it and follow the track straight ahead.

After some distance it swings to the right and ends at a gate. Leave the track to go to the left of the gate. This will bring you to a second gate in the field fence. Go through it and turn sharp left to pass between a tumulus and the fence. This will lead you to a track which goes down the hill. It passes through a gate and on down the hillside from which there are yet more good views of Weymouth and Portland.

About halfway down the hill the track leads through another gate and divides. Take the right-hand branch. It runs along the ridge of the gully through which the middle branch passes and quickly degenerates into a path.

Near the end of the ridge turn right and go down the slope to a stile in the hedge. Cross the stile and follow the narrow path that runs obliquely across the field to a second stile, beyond which is the joiner's yard. Go through the yard and turn right to follow the track back to where you left the car.

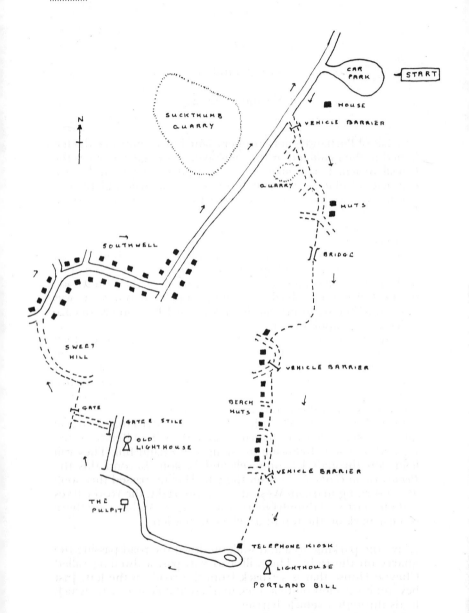

N

START

CAR PARK

HOUSE

VEHICLE BARRIER

SUCKTHUMB QUARRY

QUARRY

HUTS

BRIDGE

SOUTHWELL

SWEET HILL

VEHICLE BARRIER

BEACH HUTS

GATE

GATE & STILE

OLD LIGHTHOUSE

VEHICLE BARRIER

THE PULPIT

TELEPHONE KIOSK

LIGHTHOUSE

PORTLAND BILL

PORTLAND

WALK 21

★

4 miles (6 km)

OS Landranger 194

The Isle of Portland is not a proper island but a peninsula which is joined to the mainland by the long strip of shingle known as the Chesil Beach. It is unlike any other part of Dorset and has a character all of its own. Virtually no trees grow on its high plateau and the surface of the land is pitted with the quarries from which the famous Portland stone is extracted.

Portland Bill is the southern tip of the peninsula. It has an impressive rugged coastline where layers of limestone rock shelve down to the sea. There are caves here and three lighthouses. The youngest, which was built in 1905, is still in use and is often open to the public. The older of the two lighthouses on the eastern side of the Bill is now a bird observatory and field centre. It was opened by the naturalist Sir Peter Scott in 1961 and visitors are welcome by appointment.

Towards the northern end of Portland is an old prison which was later used as a borstal training centre. During the Victorian era convicts from this prison built the great breakwaters that enclose Portland harbour. This is one of the largest and safest naval bases in the world and a great variety of Royal Naval craft are to be seen in the waters around Portland.

From Weymouth follow the road signs to Portland. This will take you along the road that runs along the Chesil Beach. At the far end of it start following the signs to Portland Bill. They will lead you through Fortuneswell and Easton. Beyond this the *Pennsylvania Castle Hotel* is on the left. Having passed this hotel and a turning marked 'Weston ½' on the right, the road curves right to skirt Suckthumb Quarry on the right. At this point there is a car park on the top of a hillock to the left.

Leave the parking area and walk on down the road passing the quarry on the right. This will lead you past a dwelling called Cheyne House that is set back from the road on the left. Just beyond it turn left on to a track marked 'Public Footpath' which leads through a vehicle barrier.

Where the track forks keep to the left-hand branch which continues along the cliff, ignoring a quarry entrance on the right.

Not far beyond this the track forks again. Still keep to the left so that you follow the edge of the cliff. This will bring you to a group of fishermen's huts and winches.

Ignore a track to the right and another that follows the cliff to the left. Go straight ahead taking a path which climbs a slight slope and is partially blocked by a rectangular lump of stone.

The path skirts some fields to the right and crosses a drainage ditch by a narrow plank bridge, then passes another winch on the left. Beyond this it leads through a group of beach huts and joins a track that comes down from the road to the right.

Follow the track straight ahead then leave it where it swings right just beyond the vehicle barrier and carry on towards the red and white lighthouse. This is the newest of the lighthouses.

Ignore a second track to the right and go on to reach a gravel track. Follow this straight ahead ignoring two tracks to the right and where it turns abruptly right beside a stone block marked 'Private property Tenants cars only' leave it to pass a vehicle barrier on the left and cross the grass to the telephone kiosk.

This telephone kiosk stands beside the turning circle where the road ends at Portland Bill and it is a good idea to abandon the walk for a short time at this point to explore the Bill itself. Beyond the lighthouse are impressive cliffs where shelves of rock provide convenient seats on which to sit and admire the view. Pulpit Rock is to the right and marks the very southernmost tip of Portland. It is a tall rectangular block of limestone against which rests a slab provided with footholds.

Continue the walk by going back to the turning circle and walking up the road, passing the car park on your left. The road swings left by *The Pulpit* public house and then right to pass the old lighthouse on the right. Just beyond it turn left on to a track marked 'Public Footpath'.

Where the track meets a path in a T-junction at the top of the hill take the right-hand branch. It leads through a gate and on along the hilltop to where it is joined by a grassy track from the right and swings left to widen into a track. Follow it round to the left. It is now bordered by stone walls and straight ahead the old Victorian prison can be seen on the horizon.

Where the track joins a road turn right. Follow the road round to the right and at the junction take the right-hand fork passing The Old Police House on the right. You are now in Southwell Street.

At the next junction follow the road round to the left. It is signposted 'Easton 1½, Weymouth 8'. This will bring you back past the quarry on the left to the car park on the right.

MAIDEN CASTLE
AND FOUR BARROW HILL

WALK 22

★

6½ miles (10 km)

OS Landranger 194

Situated high on a hill one mile south of the county town of Dorchester, Maiden Castle is one of the largest and most formidable hill forts in England. It was built over 2,000 years ago and incorporated a smaller early Iron Age village which was protected by a single rampart and ditch.

Take the A354 from Dorchester travelling towards Weymouth and turn right on to the road signposted to Maiden Castle. Follow the road to its end and park in the car park at the foot of the hill fort.

Start the walk by going back along the road for about 400 yards to where a track leads away to the left. Turn on to this and follow it up a slight slope, passing a round barrow in the field on the right.

Not far beyond this barrow the track is crossed by another and then passes through a gate. Ignore the cross track and carry straight on through the gate to reach a farm just over the brow of the hill.

A track leads away through a gate to the right near the farm but disregard it and carry on, passing a house on the right and going through a gate straight ahead to enter the farmyard. Here the track turns left to skirt a farm building on the right and then swings right beside it at a point where another track leads straight ahead.

Follow the track round to the right. It passes another house on the left and then forks. Take the right-hand branch and then turn left almost immediately to pass through a gate on to an unmetalled track which cuts between a concrete block building on the left and some silos on the right.

The track passes another round barrow in a field on the left and then descends a slope, skirts a group of houses on the right and emerges on to the road. Turn left and follow the road to the junction, then go right and almost immediately left to take a lane labelled 'Private entrance, Eweleaze Barn and Dairy only'.

The lane ascends a steep hill and then flattens out to follow the ridge. From here there are very good views across the rolling

69

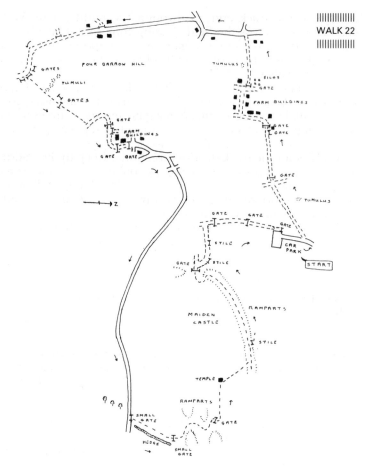

countryside to the west of Dorchester and the tall chimney-like shape of the monument erected to the memory of Admiral Sir Thomas Masterman Hardy, who sailed with Lord Nelson, is to be seen on the skyline.

After some distance the lane passes between some farm buildings on the left and a bungalow on the right and then degenerates into a metalled track. Ignore a track which leads through a gate on the right near the bungalow and carry straight on.

Once the farm buildings are left behind a whole row of round barrows will be seen on the horizon straight ahead. The track soon becomes unmetalled and a secondary track passes through a gate on the right. Disregard it and keep to the main track.

This will bring you to a place where the track turns left and then swings right again at a point where there are three gates on the left. Leave the track and go through the middle gate. Walk diagonally left across the field, passing four round barrows on your left, to reach two more gates in the opposite corner. Go through the right-hand one and head down the slope to reach a track in the valley.

Turn left on to this track and follow it down to the farm. There is a track on the left just before the first farm building but ignore this. The main track goes through a gate and then curves to the left, skirting some farm buildings on the left and passing through two more gates to reach the farmhouse.

At this point the track divides three ways. Keep to the middle branch which passes the farmhouse on the right and some cottages on the left before joining the road. Turn left to follow the road for a short distance before turning right on to a lane signposted 'Winterborne Monkton 1¼'.

Where the lane is joined by another from the left and a farm entrance on the right, go straight on. The lane turns sharply to the right and then winds through a valley.

After about ½ mile it is approached by a line of trees on the right and, not far beyond this, a hedge runs down the hillside on the left. Just before this hedge meets the road there is a small gate in the fence on the left. Go through this and follow the footpath up the slope to another small gate on the ridge. This will bring you to the edge of Maiden Castle.

Take the grassy path straight ahead which leads up on to the ramparts. At the top of the first rise it swings slightly left and then curves right, passing a stone wall set into the bank on the left.

Beyond this the path turns left again to cut through another rampart. On the far side turn sharp right to go through a small gate with a large gate beside it and then bear slightly left to climb the slope, passing two notice boards on the left and heading for another at the top of the rise. This board marks the position of the Roman temple.

Bear diagonally right from the temple to reach the narrow path that runs along the top of the inner rampart and follow it round to the left. After a short distance a path which starts at a stile leads down into the ditch on the right. Ignore this and carry on along the ridge to reach the place where the rampart ends at the hill fort's main entrance. From here there is a good view of the complex pattern of ramparts which guard this important point.

Turn left to descend the rampart and then sharp right through a small gate that opens on to a gravel path. Ignore a grassy path which leads straight ahead and follow the gravel path round to the right.

Keep to the path, passing two stiles on the right and where the path joins a track, turn right. The track runs down a slope through three sets of gates to reach the car park.

SHERBORNE DEER PARK

WALK 23

★

3 miles (4.5 km)

OS Landranger 183

For those who want a real taste of country life this walk is superb. Parts of it lead through the grounds of Sherborne Castle. This magnificent country house was built by Sir Walter Raleigh but later became the property of the Digby family. Its park was laid out by 'Capability' Brown and does great credit to his genius.

Pinford is one of the farms on the estate. It is surrounded by fields in which flocks of geese are to be seen. From here the route leads through the park where herds of deer graze beneath the trees. They often pause at what they consider a reasonable distance to watch the passer-by, rather than diving for cover at the first signs of approach, and so the chance of getting a good view of them is very high.

This can be rather a wet walk and waterproof footwear is strongly recommended for all but the longest spells of dry weather.

Take the A30 out of Sherborne heading towards Shaftesbury and just on the outskirts of Milborne Port turn right on to a road signposted to Goathill. Where the road forks ¼ mile beyond Goathill take the left-hand branch which is marked 'Stourton Caundle'. Drive up the hill and park in the lay-by on the left under the trees.

Walk back down the road and at the junction bear to the right following the sign to Goathill. Carry on until you come to the church on the left and turn left beside it on to a track marked 'Footpath Pinford 1'.

Go straight ahead, passing some cottages on the left and some farm buildings on the right, to leave the farmyard by a gate at the far side. Follow the track past the duck pond on your left. The track then bears slightly right and is crossed by another which comes down a slope from the right. Ignore this and go straight ahead through a gate.

Leave the track and bear left to follow the fence round the edge of the field until you come to a gate which leads into the wood on the left. At this point turn right and cross the field to another gate on the far side. Go through it and turn left. This brings you

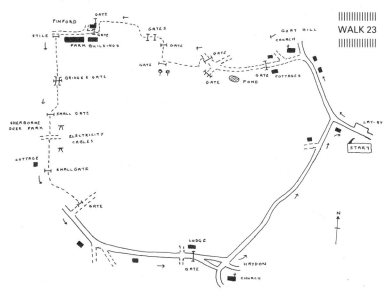

almost immediately to two gates set one in front of the other. Pass through both of these and turn right to follow the fence along two sides of the field. Ignore a gate in the corner of the field and turn left, passing a wooden silage store on the right. At the end of it turn right to pass between it and some farm buildings on the left to reach a gate.

Beyond the gate follow the track straight ahead to pass the farmhouse on the left. Just beyond it turn left over a stile and cross the field keeping the farmhouse and the duck pond on your left. This will bring you to a small gate on a bridge. Go through it and straight on along the side of the next field to a second gate in the wall at the top. Beyond this is the deer park.

A set of electricity cables supported by wooden poles crosses the park at this point. From the gate go straight ahead, keeping these cables on the left as you ascend the slope. Halfway up the path is crossed by a track. Ignore it and carry straight on.

At the top of the slope there is a gamekeeper's cottage on the right. Go straight ahead through a narrow gate which marks the boundary of the deer park and follow the fence on the left. This will bring you to where a gate opens on to a track at the corner of the field. Go through the gate and turn right.

The track meets a metalled drive in a T-junction. Turn left and follow the drive round to the left, ignoring two tracks which join it from the right.

The drive leads down through the park gates to the road. Turn left and follow the road until you come to a junction on the right marked 'Stourton Caundle'. Turn right here and walk back up the hill to where you left the car.

CERNE ABBAS AND
UP CERNE

WALK 24

★

4 miles (6 km)

OS Landranger 194

Cerne Abbas was once a thriving market and manufacturing town but its industry died during the 19th century when it was bypassed by the railway. Today all that remains is a beautiful village which must be one of the most interesting in Dorset.

As its name suggests, Cerne Abbas once had a large abbey. It was a Benedictine foundation and was originally built in about AD 987 by Ethelmaer, Earl of Cornwall. During the 11th century it was rebuilt on a lavish scale and became one of the richest abbeys in Dorset, owning land as far away as Brownsea Island in Poole Harbour. It was also an important monastic school.

All this came to an end in 1539 when King Henry VIII had the abbey dissolved. Within 40 years it was in ruins and today little remains except some humps in Beavoir meadow and the beautiful porch to the abbot's hall which stands in the grounds of the manor house. This house is owned by the Digby family and was used, together with the arched gateway to the graveyard, as part of the setting for the film *Tom Jones*.

In the far corner of the graveyard is St Augustine's Well. It is a wishing well and is said to have been struck by St Augustine with the words 'Cerno Deum'. A short distance from the manor house stands the ancient church with its interesting corbels, and directly opposite it is a fine terrace of late medieval houses.

By far the most interesting thing to be seen in Cerne Abbas must surely be the Cerne Abbas Giant. This is the large figure of a man carved into the side of the hill just north of the village. It is very old and was probably intended to represent an early British fertility god. Up Cerne is a charming little hamlet with a beautiful manor house which dates from about 1600.

Take the A352 Sherborne road from Dorchester. When the road enters Cerne Abbas carry straight on until you reach the decontrol signs at the far end of Acreman Street. Just beyond this point there is a turning on the right marked 'Village Centre & Toilets'. Turn right here and follow the road for a short distance down the hill before turning left into a lane signposted 'Picnic Area 65 yds'. Park in the picnic area on the left.

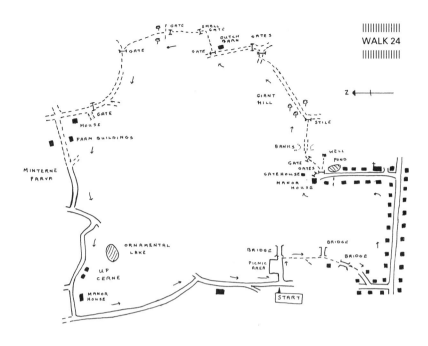

Leave the picnic area and turn left to walk towards the bridge but just before it swing right on to a path which borders the stream. Ignore a path that leads down to the children's playground on the right and carry straight on to where the path forks. Take the right-hand branch. It passes a house on the right and then crosses a narrow bridge over the mill race to reach an unmetalled lane.

Where the lane joins the road turn left and then left again at the T-junction to follow the main village street to where it widens near *The Royal Oak* public house. Turn left again here into Abbey Street. At this point the church is on the right and the medieval houses on the left.

Walk up Abbey Street to the manor house. Just before it there is a duck pond on the right which borders the churchyard. At this point it is possible to take an interesting short diversion. To the left is the entrance to the manor house garden and, for a small fee, visitors are allowed into it to see the impressive abbey gateway.

To continue the walk go through the churchyard gate. Just inside it the path divides. The right-hand branch runs along beside the churchyard wall to St Augustine's Well, which it is also worth taking a short detour to visit, but to carry on with the walk follow the left-hand branch. It runs obliquely across the churchyard to another arched gateway that gives access to a meadow.

Turn right and walk across the grass to take a track which leads up a slope between two banks towards the trees.

At the top of the slope the track becomes faint. Carry straight on keeping the trees on the left to reach a stile at the far side of the field. Cross the stile and turn left on to a grassy track, ignoring a path which climbs a slope to the left.

The track runs along the foot of the hill for some distance before beginning to climb. Near the top of the slope it degenerates into a path and becomes indistinct but carry straight on keeping the gully on your left. This will bring you to a place where the path joins a track. Turn right and follow the track to a gate beside a cattle pen.

Go through the gate and sharp left through a second gate with a small gate beside it on to a track. Walk along this until you reach a Dutch barn on the right. In front of it is a gate. Turn right through this gate and walk past the barn.

Follow the hedge on the left. This will eventually bring you to a small gate on the left. Go through it and head slightly right down the hill to a gate on the far side of the field.

Beyond this a path runs parallel to the fence. Ignore it and take a rather indistinct path which goes down the slope through a clump of trees. When it emerges from the trees it leads straight on to skirt a hedge on the left at the bottom of the slope. This will bring you to a gate set in the hedge.

Turn left through it and go straight across the field beyond to reach a track in the valley. Walk along the track and where it merges with another from the left carry straight on, keeping the hedge on the left.

The track leads through a gate and swings right to pass a house on the left. Not far beyond this it is crossed by another track. Turn left here. The track passes some farm buildings and then widens into a metalled lane which leads to the road.

At the road turn left and walk round the bend to where a lane to Up Cerne leads away to the right. Take this lane. It climbs initially and then descends a slope passing the ornamental lake on the left.

Having passed some cottages on the left the road forks. Take the left-hand branch which leads straight ahead with the manor house behind a hedge on the left.

This will bring you to where the lane swings left and is joined by a track from the right. Keep to the lane, and when it eventually joins the road turn right. This will take you past the old workhouse, which is now a nursing home, on the right and the viewpoint for the giant on the left. Just beyond this the lane runs down to the village. Follow it for a short distance and then turn left to reach the picnic area where you left the car.

FLEET

WALK 25

★

3½ miles (5.5 km)

OS Landranger 194

To anybody who has read John Meade Falkner's famous novel *Moonfleet* the tiny hamlet of East Fleet needs no introduction. Yet little remains of the original village in which the story was set. On 23rd November 1824 there was a terrific storm. It blew a 90 ton sloop, the *Ebenezer*, on to the crest of the Chesil Beach and caused a mighty tidal wave which tore through the village destroying the cottages and demolishing all but the chancel of the fine old church. A new church was built between the years 1827 and 1829 at the expense of the vicar, George Gould, and for some time the old building remained a neglected ruin. It has now been restored and is in the care of the Dorset Historic Churches Trust. Beneath it the Mohun family vault is still in existence together with the old smugglers' passage that connects it to the Fleet and on either side of the altar there are memorial brasses belonging to the Mohuns. The church also contains a small plaque to the memory of John Meade Falkner.

The Fleet is a narrow salt-water lake that separates the mainland from the Chesil Beach. It is a shallow stretch of tidal water containing a great amount of seaweed and is not good for swimming. It does, however, support large numbers of fish such as bass, mullet and eels which are exploited by the local fishermen.

The Chesil Beach is a barrier of stone which connects the Isle of Portland to the mainland. It is over 17 miles in length and the size of the stones increases as it goes east. At the western end it is composed of a fine shingle whilst in the east some of the stones are as big as saucers.

The Chesil Beach has been the graveyard of many a fine sailing ship. Some, such as the *Ebenezer*, were lost in storms but others were deliberately lured to their deaths by wreckers who made a handsome living from plundering vessels smashed on the Chesil stones.

Take the B3157 from Weymouth and turn left at the small roundabout in Chickerell on to a road marked 'Fleet ½'. Drive along the road for approximately a mile. Having passed the church and two dwellings on the right the road curves slightly

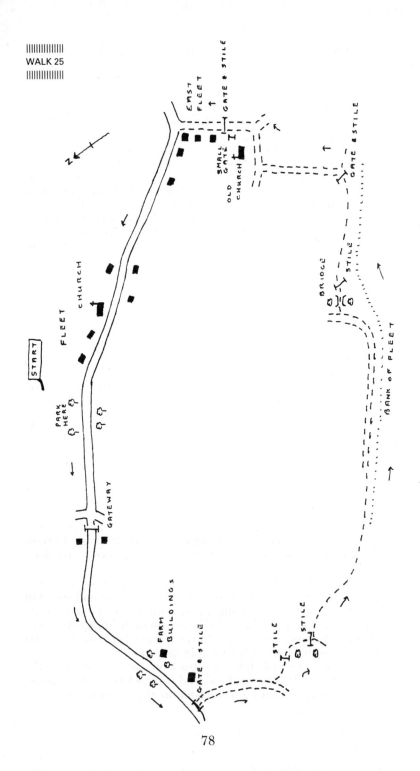

78

left. Just beyond this there are several parking places available under the trees on the right.

Walk on up the road and where it divides three ways keep to the central branch. This leads through a gateway with a lodge on either side and on down a slope from which there is a view of the sea straight ahead.

Near the bottom of the slope the road runs through a wood which screens some farm buildings on the left-hand side and then passes a red brick house on the left. Just beyond this, as the road swings right towards the *Moonfleet Hotel*, a track signposted 'to coastal path' leads through a metal field gate to the left.

Follow the track across the field and just before it passes through the fence on the far side turn left. Keeping the fence on your right walk diagonally left across the corner of the field to reach a stile at the edge of the bushes. Beyond this a narrow path skirts the wood on the right to reach a second stile, on the far side of which the path divides. Take the left-hand fork signposted 'Weymouth, East Fleet'.

This path runs along the edge of the Fleet and gives a good view of Chesil Beach on the far side of the water. Within a short distance the towering cliffs of the Isle of Portland can also be seen on the horizon straight ahead.

After about ¼ mile the fence on the left comes to an end. Carry straight on following the wide grassy track which borders the Fleet. This will bring you to a place where the expanse of water widens. The track bears left to continue along the bank for a short distance and then swings away up the hillside.

Leave the track at this point and take a narrow path which goes through a clump of bushes beside the water. The path leads across a narrow wooden bridge to reach a stile. Cross the stile and turn sharp right to follow the fence.

Go through the gate at the far side of the field and turn left to follow a track marked 'East Fleet & Church', disregarding a path to Weymouth on the right. Near the churchyard wall the track is joined by another from the left. Ignore it and turn right to cross the stream by a narrow bridge, following the signpost 'East Fleet, Chickerell'.

Just beyond the stream the track forks. Keep to the left-hand branch which follows the churchyard wall to a gate and stile. On the far side of the stile a small gate to the left opens into the churchyard. The little chapel to be seen amongst the gravestones is all that remains of the village church featured in Falkner's novel and a visit to it makes a worthwhile diversion.

To continue the walk, follow the track on past the cottages to the road and turn left. The road will lead you back to the car passing the new church, which was completed in 1829, on the way.

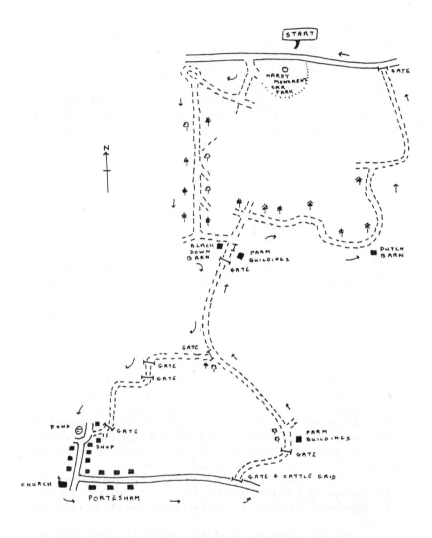

START

HARDY
MONUMENT
CAR
PARK

GATE

N

BLACK
DOWN
BARN

FARM
BUILDINGS

GATE

DUTCH
BARN

GATE

GATE

GATE

POND

SHOP

GATE

FARM
BUILDINGS

GATE

CHURCH

PORTESHAM

GATE & CATTLE GRID

THE HARDY MONUMENT

WALK 26

★

4 miles (6 km)

OS Landranger 194

The Hardy Monument stands high on the slopes of Black Down. It was erected in 1844 to the memory of Admiral Sir Thomas Masterman Hardy who was captain of Nelson's flagship, the *Victory*, during the Battle of Trafalgar.

One of the most outstanding features of this walk is the scenery. Although the flight of steps which once gave access to the platform at the top of the Hardy Monument is now closed, there are still magnificent views to be seen from the heathland at its base and from several other vantage points throughout the route. On a clear day the walker can enjoy a panorama that includes Weymouth, Portland, the Chesil Beach and St Catherine's Chapel at Abbotsbury.

Take the A35 trunk road towards Bridport from Dorchester and turn left in Winterbourne Abbas on to the Martinstown road, then turn right to follow the signs to the Hardy Monument. Around the base of the monument there is a wide expanse of open ground which provides plenty of free parking.

Near the point where the track which gives access to the open ground around the monument joins the road, a secondary track leads down the hill to the right. Take this track. Within less than a hundred yards it forks. Keep to the right-hand fork which almost immediately joins another track at a point where a path labelled 'West Bexington 6' leads straight ahead. Turn right and follow this track. It curves gently to the right and eventually ends in a circle bordering the road. Turn left at this point on to another track leading down the hill through a wood.

Close to the bottom of the first steep slope a path joins the track from the left and, not far beyond this, the track divides. Keep to the right-hand branch which goes on down the hill through the trees.

As it emerges from the wood the track forks again. Take the right-hand branch and where the track forks a third time take the left-hand branch passing a signpost on your right. This will bring you to where the track divides near some farm buildings. Turn right to follow the track through a gate and up a slope.

Near the top a track leads through a gate on the right beside a small wood. Turn right on to this. After bordering a wall on the left for some distance it passes through a gateway and continues to follow the wall down a slope towards a second gate. At this point there is a fine view of St Catherine's Chapel at Abbotsbury on the horizon to the right.

Beyond this gate the track swings right to curve round the perimeter of the field and descend the hill by some small trees on the far side. This leads you to a gate in the bottom right-hand corner of the field. It gives access to a gravel track. Where this divides keep to the right-hand branch which runs down between some houses to the road.

Turn left and follow the road through Portesham village bearing left at the shop into Front Street. At this point it is worth taking a short diversion to the right into Back Street where there is a pond on the right containing a shoal of magnificent trout. Then continue along Front Street and take the first turning on the left. This is Winters Lane. It is signposted 'Coryates, Friar Waddon, Upwey'.

Winters Lane climbs up a hill out of the village. Just where it flattens out a metalled track leads over a cattle grid to the left. It is marked 'Bridleway Hardy's Monument 1½'. Go through the metal gate beside the cattle grid and follow the track up the slope. Ignore a footpath which leads through a gate to the right at the top of the slope and carry on along the track to pass through another metal gate and skirt Portesham Farm buildings on the right.

Near the far corner of the farm buildings the track is joined by another from the right. Ignore it and carry straight on. After breasting the ridge the track leads down the hill to Black Down Barn. Here it goes through another gate and forks.

Take the right-hand fork. It leads up the hill and at the top of the primary slope is crossed by a second track. Turn right and follow this track which goes straight along the side of the hill between fir trees to the left and open fields to the right.

After some distance the track swings round in a sharp loop and then passes a Dutch barn on the right. Beyond this it turns to the left to head towards the Hardy Monument which stands on the sky-line.

The track goes straight ahead for some distance and then merges with another from the left. Turn right and follow this down a gentle slope, pausing at the bottom to admire the beautiful views of Weymouth and Portland to the right at the point where the track swings left.

Continue to follow the track through the valley to where it joins the road. Turn left and walk up the hill to the monument and the parking area.

TENANTS HILL

WALK 27

★

3½ miles (5.5 km)

OS Landranger 194

On the summit of Tenants Hill there is one of the few stone circles to be found in Dorset. This is known as Kingstone Russell Stone Circle. It can boast none of the magnificent trilithons to be found at Stonehenge and the stones that mark its circumference are not as big as those at Avebury but it is still an interesting site. It was constructed almost 4,000 years ago by the Beaker Folk. The Beaker Folk were a farming people who came to England from central Europe and gained their name from the beautiful bell-shaped beakers in which they buried the cremated remains of their dead.

This walk also provides excellent views of the village of Abbotsbury which, as its name suggests, was once the site of a large Benedictine monastery. The great barn that once belonged to it is still to be seen to the south of the church and high on a hill to the west of the village is St Catherine's Chapel.

Abbotsbury stands at the western end of the Fleet, a stretch of salt water divided from the sea by a massive bank of pebbles known as the Chesil Beach. This runs from Bridport in the west to the Isle of Portland in the east.

Bordering the car park is an old lime-kiln. Kilns such as this were once common in the chalk and limestone areas of Dorset. The lime produced from them was used for a variety of purposes such as soil improvement, the production of mortar and whitewash and the cleansing of hides for tanning. The lime was made by filling the kiln from the top with alternate layers of rock and fuel. This was allowed to burn very slowly, thus transforming the rock into lime which was then raked out at the bottom.

Take the B3157 from Weymouth travelling towards Bridport and, on the outskirts of Abbotsbury, having passed the *Swan Inn* on the left, take the first turning on the right opposite the public car park. At the T-junction turn right again and follow the lane for ½ mile to where Bishop's Limekiln Picnic Area is on the left.

Start the walk by turning left out of the car park and then almost immediately left again on to a track which leads up to a gate and stile. Beyond this bear left to follow the grassy track that runs along the base of the hill.

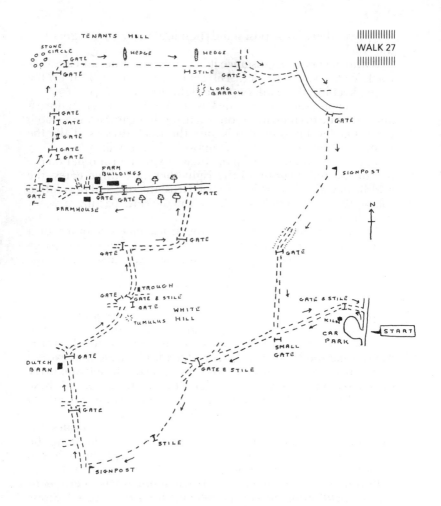

Ignore another grassy track marked 'White Hill' that leads up the slope to the right and also a small gate to the left and continue to follow the track straight ahead. This will afford you some good views of Abbotsbury in the valley to the left. The abbey barn is to be seen behind the church with the waters of the Fleet and the Chesil Beach beyond them whilst, further to the west, the impressive bulk of St Catherine's Chapel dominates the skyline.

Eventually the track merges with another from the right and runs down a slight slope to a gate with a stile beside it. On the far side of this gate the track divides. Take the left-hand branch for a short distance and then head obliquely left across the valley to reach a stile in the fence on the far side of the field. Cross this and go straight ahead, keeping the fence on your left, until you come

84

to a place where a signpost stands beside a track. Turn right on to the track.

Within a very short distance it becomes indistinct and another track leads away to the left. Disregard this and carry on up the slope, keeping the bank on your right, to reach a gate.

Just beyond the gate the track is crossed by another. Ignore it and continue to climb until you reach another gate beside a Dutch barn. On the far side of this gate the track divides. Take the right-hand branch which is signposted 'White Hill'.

The track winds its way up the final slope to join another on the top of the hill. Slightly to the right there are three gates, the middle of which has a stile beside it. Cross the stile and bear left to follow the track beside the fence on the left, passing a water trough on the right.

At the far side of the field the track meets another in a T-junction. Turn right on to this. It runs along beside the hedge and then swings left to go through a gate and descend a slope towards a wood. At the bottom of the slope the track goes through another gate and joins a lane. Turn left to follow the lane through the wood.

At the far end of the trees the lane passes through two gates near some farm buildings on the right and then degenerates into a track. This skirts the farmhouse on the left and divides three ways. Take the left-hand branch which leads straight ahead.

Ignore a track which leads down to a gate on the left and carry on to pass some cottages on the right. Beside the last one of these the track is barred by a gate. Go through it and turn sharp right to follow the garden fence up the hillside.

Where the fence ends carry straight on to reach two gates. Go through the left one and follow the fence on the right on up the slope. Ignore two gates on the right and go through one in the top right-hand corner of the field.

Beyond it carry straight on to reach another gate. This opens on to a field on the top of the hill and Kingstone Russell Stone Circle is situated a short distance to the left. The 18 stones which mark its circumference lie on their backs in the grass and are sometimes difficult to see from the gate but the position of the monument is easily seen by the English Heritage sign that has been erected within the circle.

To continue the walk, cross the corner of the field to pass through a wooden gate and then follow the hedge on the right. The path passes through a gap in the hedge on the far side of the field and then borders a second field to reach a similar gap in the next hedge, beside which is a notice bearing the legend 'Danger Low Flying Aircraft'.

Just before this notice a stile set in the hedge on the right gives access to another interesting feature which may be seen by making a very short diversion from the intended route. This is a long barrow called The Grey Mare and Her Colts that lies in a field near the crest of the hill. To see it cross the stile and, ignoring a gate in the corner of the field, follow the fence on the left to reach a second gate. The long barrow is just on the far side of it in the field on the left.

Retrace your steps to the stile, and beyond it, turn sharp right to pass the warning notice on your left and skirt the field. Be sure to obey the notice by keeping close to the hedge on the right for this is the route of the bridlepath.

Pass through a small gate beside a field gate at the far side of the field on to a track and follow it to the right. It soon merges with another from the right and runs down to the lane.

Turn right and follow the lane, ignoring a footpath marked 'Hardy Monument' which leads across a field to the left. Where the lane swings left go through a gate straight ahead on to a track signposted 'Inland Route W Bexington 3½'. The track leads up a slight slope and then becomes more indistinct. Leave it and bear slightly left to reach a signpost by the fence.

From the signpost head diagonally right across the next field following the direction indicated by the arm marked 'Bridleway Abbotsbury 1'. This will take you across a track which goes to a rubbish dump and, within a very few yards the waters of the Fleet and the Chesil Beach will become visible on the horizon straight ahead. Walk steadily towards them and you will reach the end of an old sunken track that leads down to a gate.

Beyond the gate follow the track straight ahead. It soon becomes faint but the gully through which it once ran goes on down the hillside to reach a small gate in the fence. Do not go through the gate. Turn left just before it on to a track that runs along the base of the slope. This will lead you back to the gate and stile which give access to the lane and the car park on the right.

GOLDEN CAP

WALK 28

★

3 ½ miles (5.5 km)

OS Landranger 193

Golden Cap is the highest cliff on the south coast. It is 617 ft high and forms part of a piece of coastline that is owned by the National Trust. This is a particularly lovely area and the summit of Golden Cap makes a very good vantage point from which to enjoy its beauty.

The cliffs are especially worthy of mention for no two are alike. Greensand, limestone and clay combine to give them an endless variety of colours and shades. Yet, even amongst such a wealth of colouring, Golden Cap stands out because of its unique beauty.

A small village called Stanton St Gabriel once nestled in the valley behind Golden Cap but today all that remains are a couple of thatched cottages and a ruined church. The village became isolated when the coastal road was re-routed in 1825 and the old bridge at Seatown fell into disuse, and thus the inhabitants slowly began to move away.

On the top of Golden Cap there is a memorial stone to the Earl of Antrim KBE who, for many years, was Chairman of the National Trust. It is worth pausing to study this stone, not only for the inscription but also for the fine collection of fossils embedded in the stone itself.

Take the A35 trunk road from Bridport travelling towards Lyme Regis. Turn left just before you come to the dual carriageway at the top of the hill beyond Chideock and then almost immediately left again on to the metalled track to Langdon Hill. Where the track branches take the right-hand fork. This will lead you up to the car park.

Leave the car park by the gate on the right-hand side and follow the track. It curves round the hillside and then emerges from the trees for a short distance, giving good views of the coast towards Lyme Regis. At this point it is joined by a track which comes up the slope on the right. Disregard this and carry straight on, passing a bench on the right. Ignore a track which comes down the hill on the left and keep to the main track until it curves left again and passes a seat on the right. Just beyond this turn right and then left on to a narrow path signposted 'To Coast Path, Golden Cap'.

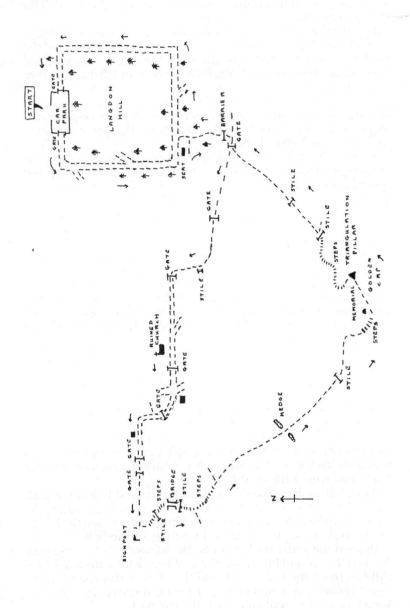

Go through the gap at the bottom of the slope and turn right through a gate into a field. Head obliquely right to a gate in the hedge at the far side and then follow the path straight ahead. This is signposted 'Bridleway St Gabriels'.

Initially the path borders the fence on the left but, as the fence veers slightly left, it diverges from it to cut across the corner of the field to a stile. Do not cross the stile, turn right beside it and descend the slope to reach a gate in the bottom left-hand corner of the field.

Go through the gate and follow the path straight ahead. It quickly broadens into a track, then runs down a slope and is joined by another track from the left. Ignore this and carry on to pass the ruined church on your right.

Beyond the church the track leads through a gate and down to St Gabriel's House where it meets three other tracks. Take the one straight ahead which goes down a slight slope and through a gate. It is joined by a footpath to the right and then swings left to pass the front of St Gabriel's Cottage. From this point continue to follow the path straight ahead, ignoring two gates on the right. This will bring you to a gate at the far side of the field which is connected by a short fenced path to a second gate. Go through these and follow the hedge on the left to a signpost.

Turn left on to the path marked 'Golden Cap ¾, Seatown 1¾'. This descends some steps into a gully. Cross the bridge over the stream and the stile beyond to reach the place where the path divides halfway up the steps on the far side. Keep to the left and carry on climbing.

At the top of the steps take the path straight ahead to the top of the primary slope, ignoring a path to the left. Then follow the edge of the cliff on your right up towards Golden Cap.

Where the path passes through a hedge take the left-hand fork and continue the climb to a stile at the top of the field. From here a path leads up to the summit.

At the top it is worth taking a short pause to enjoy the magnificent views before turning left to follow the path to a triangulation pillar. This will lead you past the memorial to the Earl of Antrim KBE on the left.

Turn left again at the triangulation pillar and follow the path down some steps to a stile. Go over this and, ignoring a path to the right, cross the field to a second stile. Cross it and follow the hedge on the right down to a gate in the corner of the field.

Beyond the gate turn left round the barrier to follow the path marked 'Langdon Hill' up the slope. Where it joins the track turn right to reach the main track and then follow this round to the right. Ignore a secondary track that leads down to the right and keep straight on until you reach the car park.

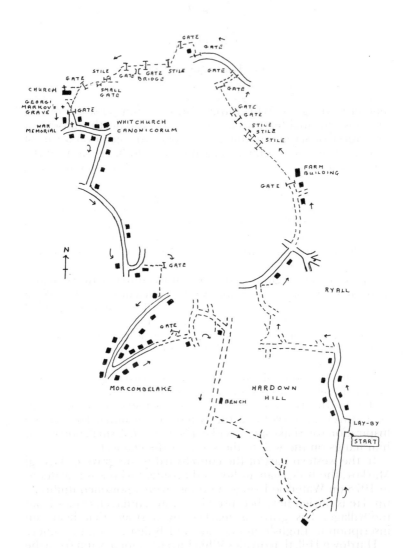

WALK 29

CHURCH

GATE

GEORGI
MARKOV'S
GRAVE

WAR
MEMORIAL

GATE

STILE

SMALL
GATE

GATE
BRIDGE

GATE STILE

WHITCHURCH
CANONICORUM

GATE

GATE

GATE

GATE

STILE
STILE

STILE

FARM
BUILDING

GATE

RYALL

N

GATE

GATE

MORCOMBELAKE

HARDOWN
HILL

BENCH

LAY-BY

START

WHITCHURCH CANONICORUM

WALK 29

★

3 miles (4.5 km)

OS Landranger 193

The little village of Whitchurch Canonicorum possesses one of the most unusual features in England. In the north transept of the church of St Candida and Holy Cross is the medieval shrine of St Wite. It is one of only two such shrines to have survived the Reformation, the other being that of Edward the Confessor in Westminster Abbey.

The identity of St Wite is something of a mystery. Some say that she was a Saxon woman who was killed during a Danish raid on the coast, others that she is really St Blanche and that her relics were brought to Dorset from Brittany during the early years of the 10th century when a number of Bretons came to live in the area.

Up until the beginning of the 20th century a third theory advocated that St Wite was not a woman but a monk named Witta who went with St Boniface to Germany where they were killed and their bodies brought back to England for burial. This theory was proved erroneous, however, in 1900 when the shrine was repaired and the lead box inside the stone coffin opened to reveal the bones of a woman.

Besides the body of the saint there are two other interesting burials in Whitchurch Canonicorum. Beneath the floor of the vestry lie the remains of Sir George Somers, an Elizabethan adventurer who colonised the island of Bermuda. He was the inspiration for Shakespeare's play *The Tempest*. A small portrait of him hangs on the wall to the south of the chancel.

In the western part of the churchyard is the grave of Georgi Markov, the Bulgarian author and dissident who was murdered in 1978 on Waterloo Bridge, London, with a poisoned umbrella tip. He is buried here because his widow, Annabel, comes from the village. His grave is marked by a stone that bears an inscription in English on one side and Bulgarian on the other.

Hardown Hill, that divides Whitchurch Canonicorum from the coast, is a local beauty spot. It is owned by the National Trust and crowned by an expanse of heathland which is particularly lovely when the heather is in bloom.

Take the A35 from Bridport travelling towards Lyme Regis

and turn right on the outskirts of Morcombelake on to a lane marked 'Ryall ¾'. Drive up this lane for ¼ mile, ignoring a turning to the left, and park on the right in a lay-by flanked by oak trees and situated just before a cottage on the left.

Walk on along the lane for approximately ¼ mile, passing a path which leads up the hill on the left and another that crosses a stile on the right, to take a track on the left. This is situated just beyond a pair of cottages called Hillside Cottages and is signposted 'Bridleway Hardown Hill'.

The track forks almost immediately. Keep to the left-hand branch. It goes straight up the hillside and then forks again. Still keep to the left. Ignore a track to the left near a National Trust sign and turn sharp right on to a narrow path just beyond it.

The path, which is initially very stony, descends a slope and then forks. Take the right-hand branch. After a short distance it joins a track. Bear left to follow this on down the hill to the lane.

Where the track joins the lane a path signposted 'Byway to Ryall' leads away to the right. Ignore it and turn right on to the lane. This will take you down a hill to a place where four lanes meet. Go straight ahead on to a metalled track labelled 'Beerland Farm'.

The track leads down a slope to reach a bungalow and then a farmhouse on the right. Disregard a track marked 'footpath' that cuts between these two buildings and carry straight on through a gate which gives access to a field with some farm buildings on the right.

Bear obliquely left down the slope to reach a stile in the bottom right-hand corner of the field. Cross this and another, double stile, straight ahead then pass through two gates to follow the hedge on the right. This will bring you to a gate at the far end of the field. Beyond this turn right to reach a gate that opens on to a lane.

Turn left and follow the lane to where a gate on the right is labelled 'footpath'. Go through it and walk along beside the fence on the left to reach the end of a garden before turning left towards a second gate.

Head obliquely left across the next field to reach a stile in the far corner and then go straight ahead to pass through a gate on the far side of the field beyond. Carry on across another field ignoring a bridge which crosses the stream on the left and, having gone through a gate, follow the hedge on the left to a stile.

Cross the stile and turn right, ignoring a small gate on the left to follow the path to the entrance to the churchyard. From here the path straight ahead will lead you past the church on the right. The south door is usually open so that those who wish may take a break from the walk to look around inside.

Beyond the church the path leads on down to the gate at the

western end of the churchyard. Anybody who wants to see Georgi Markov's grave should leave it for a while to turn right beside the lamp where two paths merge and walk across the grass passing a small yew tree on the right. The author's grave is the sixth on the left and is situated just beyond a small tree.

Leave the churchyard by the gate at the western end, walk down to the war memorial and turn left. The lane leads through the village for a short distance before being joined by another on the right signposted 'Morcombelake ¾, Bridport 5'. Turn right and walk up the hill to a T-junction. Turn left and follow the lane up a slope.

At the top it is met by a lane from the left. Turn on to this but leave it almost immediately to take a path that leads straight ahead, passing between a hedge on the left and a building on the right.

Ignore a gate at the top of the slope and follow the path round to the right. It provides a good view of Charmouth and Lyme Bay on the right before passing a cottage on the right and running up a slight slope to join a lane.

Turn right to follow the lane down to the village and then sharp left on to a no through road called Love Lane. This is bordered by houses for some distance and then degenerates into a track. Carry straight on and where the track forks keep to the right-hand branch. This will bring you to a place where two tracks cross. Turn left and follow the track up the slope passing a National Trust sign on the right.

At the top of the slope the track divides. Take the right-hand fork and follow it past the building on the hilltop, ignoring a track to the left and a path to the right.

The track merges with another from the left and swings to the right. Follow it round to the right and on along the top of Hardown Hill to where a memorial bench to Charles Shipman stands amongst the heather on the left. Having passed this turn left on to a narrow path.

Where the path forks keep to the right-hand branch which cuts through a low bank and then runs on across the hilltop to join another path in a T-junction. Turn right on to this and follow it through some low bushes and down a slope to a grassy track.

Turn right on to the track which curves down the hillside and joins a metalled track. Turn left and then left again where the track meets the lane. This will take you back to where the lay-by is on the right.

STONEBARROW HILL

NATIONAL
TRUST CENTRE

GATE

PARK MERE

BARRIER

START

STILE

CAIN'S FOLLY

GATE & CATTLE GRID

BANK

GATE + STILE

SMALL GATE

SMALL GATE

GATES

GATE

GATE

GATE

GATE

GATE

UPCOT

GATE ST GABRIELS HOUSE

GATE

SIGNPOST

BROOM CLIFF

STILE

STILE

HEDGE

STILE

STILE

STILE

STILE

STILE

BRIDGE

STEPS

BRIDGE

STILE

STILE

BRIDGE

BRIDGE STILE

STILE

STILE

N

STONEBARROW HILL

WALK 30

★

4½ miles (7 km)

OS Landranger 193

The area in which this walk is situated is part of the Golden Cap Estate owned by the National Trust. It is a place of great natural beauty composed of softly rolling hills and rugged cliffs that provide magnificent views.

Parts of the estate consist of open heathland, but the majority of it is farmed. The farmers use the more traditional methods and this means that a great amount of wild-life is able to survive here. There is a wide selection of wild flowers, a large variety of birds including buzzards and kestrels, mammals such as badgers and foxes and, in summer, an abundance of brightly coloured butterflies and other insects.

Take the A35 trunk road from Bridport travelling towards Honiton and turn left at the beginning of the Charmouth bypass, following the signs 'Charmouth ¾, Catherston Leweston 1, Wootton Fitzpaine 2'. The road leads down a hill. As it swings right at the bottom turn sharp left on to a narrow lane. The lane climbs a slope, crosses a cattle grid and degenerates into an unmetalled track. There is a National Trust sign on the right with ample parking spaces just beyond it.

Begin the walk by following the track through a gate. It passes the National Trust information centre on the left and then continues along the ridge. At the place where it merges with another track from the right and then narrows to go over a cattle grid straight ahead, turn right to follow a path signposted 'Chardown Hill, St Gabriels'. This leads through a small gate.

Just beyond the gate the path forks. Take the left-hand branch which is labelled 'Chardown Hill'. It runs across the field skirting some bushes on the left, through a gate with a stile beside it and then on along the hill-top to another small gate.

Not far beyond this the path cuts through a low bank and divides. Follow the right-hand branch which curves round to the brow of the hill, then carry on down the slope and through a gateway to reach a track in the valley.

Turn left, go through another gate and follow the track past a farmhouse on the right and a cottage on the left. This will bring

95

you to a farmyard. Turn left on to a track signposted 'St Gabriels, Morcombelake 1'. This goes through the left of two farm gates and then runs between fields down a slight slope.

Where the track meets three others, turn right on to the one marked 'St Gabriels ½, Golden Cap'. This track winds down another slight slope passing a gate on the left labelled 'Parking For Campers Only' to reach a second gate marked 'No parking, Private access to St Gabriel's Cottages'. Go through this gate and follow the track down into the valley.

Having crossed St Gabriel's Bridge the track goes up a slight slope to St Gabriel's House. Here four tracks meet. Turn on to the one which leads sharply away to the right and is signposted 'to coast path'. Go through the gate and, ignoring the narrow footpath that ascends some steps to the right, walk on past St Gabriel's Cottage. Beyond this carry straight on passing two field gates on the right, to reach a gate on the far side of the field. Go through this gate which is closely followed by another at the end of a short stretch of fenced path and then follow the hedge on the left to a signpost. Turn right beside it following the sign 'Charmouth 2¼, Lyme Regis 4¼'.

Walk up the slope to go over a stile in the hedge and then turn slightly left and cross the corner of the field to a second stile. From here the path leads slightly to the right across the next field heading for a gap near the far left-hand corner of the hedge. Go through the gap and carry straight on to another stile at the top of the slope. Cross this and bear left to follow the curve of the cliff to the next stile, ignoring a gate across the field to the right.

Cross the stile and, ignoring another to the right, head straight down the hill into the gully. Here there is a bridge with a stile on the far side beyond which a flight of steps leads up out of the bushes.

At the top of the steps bear slightly right to follow the path to yet another stile and then go straight ahead down the hill keeping the edge of the cliff on the left. Cross the small stream in the valley and carry on up the next slope.

Continue along the edge of the cliff, crossing a narrow footbridge and climbing a slope to another stile beyond which is a field. Carry on across this field to a stile on the far side and then, ignoring a path to the right marked 'Smugglers Path, Stonebarrow Hill', follow the path up the hill through the bushes. It is a steep climb but well worth it as the views from the top are magnificent.

Ignore a path to the right where the bushes end at the top of the first slope and carry straight on up to the ridge.

Cross the ridge to reach a signpost and turn right beside it on to a grassy track marked 'NT information and car park ½'. The track runs beside a fence on the left and then swings left at a point where there is a cycle barrier straight ahead. Go through this barrier to reach the car park.